PRAC~~TIC~~

CW00406785

Also by Nollaig Frost:

Frost, N. (ed) (2011). *Qualitative Research Methods in Psychology: Combining Core Approaches*, Open University Press

Practising Research

Why you're always part of the research process even when you think you're not

Nollaig Frost

 macmillan education **palgrave**

First published 2016 by
PALGRAVE

Palgrave in the UK is an imprint of Macmillan Publishers Limited, registered in England, company number 785998, of 4 Crinan Street, London, N1 9XW.

Palgrave Macmillan in the US is a division of St Martin's Press LLC, 175 Fifth Avenue, New York, NY 10010.

Palgrave is a global imprint of the above companies and is represented throughout the world.

Palgrave® and Macmillan® are registered trademarks in the United States, the United Kingdom, Europe and other countries.

ISBN 978–1–137–39828–4 paperback

This book is printed on paper suitable for recycling and made from fully managed and sustained forest sources. Logging, pulping and manufacturing processes are expected to conform to the environmental regulations of the country of origin.

A catalogue record for this book is available from the British Library.

A catalog record for this book is available from the Library of Congress.

Printed and bound by CPI Group (UK) Ltd, Croydon, CR0 4YY

MIX
Paper from
responsible sources
FSC® C013604

For Nick, Sam and Leona

Contents

Acknowledgements

Acknowledging the help, support, inspiration and input toward the writing of this book means thanking many people. Some have responded directly to my requests and queries for dialogue about what it means to be a researcher, and others will not be aware that through my engagement with them, I have learnt, pondered, and realised new insights to this aspect of research practice.

The idea and initial outlines for the book came from my research practice, supervision and teaching. Realisation through my work with mothers, students, colleagues and collaborators that who the researcher is goes far beyond what she does, came variously as insightful reflections, as slow-burning ideas, and as questions to be variously dismissed, returned to and understood. Thank you to Professor Stephen Frosh and Dr Amal Treacher for being inspiring PhD supervisors who set me off on this trail. Also to my PhD students who have enabled me to aspire to follow this example. Thanks also to Professor Toni Bifulco, Professor Sasha Roseneil and Dr Rachel Shaw amongst countless other researchers who have shared ideas and thoughts so generously.

I have worked collaboratively with many researchers and in many ways and always learn something from them about the humanness of being a researcher. There are too many to name but I would like to acknowledge in particular the Pluralism in Qualitative Research (PQR) team, the Network for Pluralism in Qualitative Research (NPQR) members, my American and Irish colleagues at the International Congress of Qualitative Inquiry, in the Society for Qualitative Inquiry in Psychology, and at University College Cork, and the Qualitative Methods in Psychology (QMiP) Section of the British Psychological Society, all of whom have enabled me to develop so many new ideas and to think each time about why I am so interested in them. My colleagues at Middlesex University have always been supportive and know when to give me space and when to drag me out of my own reveries.

The book would not have been written in the timely fashion that it was without the practical support that I have had from Research Assistants, in particular, Jacqueline Napieralla, who has carried out so many tasks in enthusiastic and helpful ways, to keep the book's progress on track, often adding them to the to-do list of her own professional requirements. Thank you, too, to Priscilla Owusu for her unfailing commitment to getting this book done, to Zainab Ephrahaim for brainstorming with me about what students would like to see in it, and to Jenna Lloyd for helping me to navigate the vast body of relevant literature. Deborah Rodriguez and Frauke Elichaoff have provided practical support to my research practice in ways too numerous to mention, developed new ideas with me and sent me literature they think will be useful, all the time maintaining a consistent belief that this book could be written. I am very grateful for their help. Thanks, too, to Ruth Spence for her willingness to contribute to the book.

The book is greatly enhanced by the inclusion of interview material from senior researchers. They know who they are but I hope that they also know that I am very grateful for the time they gave up in unbelievably busy schedules to be interviewed and for the honesty, humour and wisdom that is so apparent in their words.

Paul Stevens, Isabel Berwick and Cathy Scott at Palgrave have been extremely helpful and understanding editors who have supported the work through their sound advice, encouraging words and helpful suggestions from its inception to its completion.

And, my family. Nick, Sam and Leona have lived with my research for many years. Sam and Leona are wonderfully understanding children who may not always like it but always allow me to 'get on with my writing' and this has only been possible because Nick has always been there for them, and for me. Thank you all very much. Teddie helped, too, by forcing me to leave the desk to walk her when I thought I didn't want to and enabled me to realise that these opportunities to reflect on the world around us are key to all that we do as researchers and writers. Thank you, too, to my sisters and brother, Rachel, Hannah, Tiss and Jerome, whose teasing, mickey-taking and general putting-into-perspective of this project served to spur me on to get it done. Finally, to my parents who are always supportive and always proud. It means a lot and I thank you all very much.

Nollaig Frost

The publisher and the author would like to thank Emerald Group Publishing Limited, for permission to reproduce quotes from Frost, N., & Holt, A. (2014). Mother, researcher, feminist, woman: reflections on 'maternal status' as a researcher identity. *Qualitative Research Journal*, 14(2), 90–102.

Preface

This book is about being a researcher. It considers who a researcher is, what a researcher does, what it is like to be a researcher and what these things mean for research studies. It is not a book about research methods and it is not a book about how to do research. The book is about the person or people behind the research. The person or people without whom the research would not happen.

The book has been written to discuss many questions about the impact of the researcher on research practice, the impact of research practice on the researcher and what this can all mean for what research is done, how it is carried out and how it is reported. Questions such as 'Does it make a difference that you are a mother researching motherhood? How do you know that someone else would reach the same research findings as you? How do you decide what to research and with whom?' and 'What is it like to research upsetting topics?' I have asked myself these questions, been asked them by students, discussed them with fellow researchers and sought to answer them for non-researcher friends. The book does not claim to have all the answers, nor to know all the questions but it has been written because I believe that it is important and valuable to good research ideas and good research practice to consider the questions and what they mean for researchers seeking to produce research that is not only useful and interesting to others but also credible. The book draws on personal practice (mine and that of other researchers), curiosity and insight of researchers at all levels of their research careers. It considers different research approaches and research into a wide range of topics. It aims to be useful to researchers at all stages of their research careers, and across disciplines, who have an interest in enhancing their research practice from the initial idea about what to research to the final presentation of the research, by considering their role in it.

The book is intended to start to fill a space on the platform that provides books about what to do in research. There are many books that consider this in many ways but there are many fewer that consider who it is who is doing the research and what this means across the range of research methods, approaches, designs and techniques available to researchers. This book aims to focus readers' attention on the human element behind and within research practice. The book is more than a book about reflexivity and strives to go beyond rhetoric about reflective practice to encourage researchers to consider themselves; their motivations, their intentions, their emotions, their challenges and their presence as a person in the research process.

Writing the book has been an extensive research project in itself and this final presentation has been designed so that readers can either read it through or dip in and out of chapters as they become more and less salient to their research practice. It considers objective and subjective researchers, researchers researching alone or in teams, researchers using one method or many, researchers researching topics and experiences that they have prior knowledge of and researchers researching topics and experiences that are unknown to them at the research outset.

I have been privileged to have been able to interview many researchers for their thoughts and ideas about what their research means to them and to include excerpts from these as Researcher Views throughout the book. These complement the many research examples that illustrate key points, models and ideas, with Research Examples. The Reflective Questions, Hints and Tips, and Further Reading sections in each chapter aim to enable researchers reading the book to consider how the ideas within it can be applied to their own research practice.

Once I started writing this book, the flow and progress came easily. But that was only because of all the researchers that have contributed to this book, some knowingly and others without knowing. To all, I say thank you, and to other readers I hope that the book is informative, provocative and a useful addition to your research library. If it is, I look forward to encountering new examples of thoughtful, well-considered research that has been carried out by thoughtful, considerate researchers.

Why is the researcher important?

1

The impact of the researcher

> **Researcher View**
>
> 'I had to get the train at 7.17 am from London, arriving at Cardiff at 9.44 am to start interviewing at 10 am. So that meant that I had breakfast at 6 am, and the train there didn't have any food or drink as it was a small four-carriage train. The couple I was to interview picked me up at the station, so I didn't have a chance to get anything to eat or drink before the interviews… Unfortunately, my belly decided it also had an opinion during the first interview (with the man) and started roaring really loudly! He could hear it and I felt so awkward that I had to make a comment about having had breakfast so many hours ago… (and I didn't want him to think it was anything else!). There was a plate with pastries on the table, so he asked me if I would like one, to which I just had to quickly tear off some bites and eat them really quickly in the hope that this would quieten down my belly, until I was done interviewing at least! Normally, I wouldn't say yes, and I only agree to a glass of water if they offer anything. So my belly was quiet for a while… then later on my throat made this weird musical sound when I asked a question. He must have thought I was so weird! I nipped to the loo in between the end of his interview and the start of her interview, and they were chatting when I came out and I thought he might have been telling her that I was weird, so I thought I would own it when I spoke with her and told her that it was so embarrassing in the interview with him because although I'd had an early breakfast, my belly was rumbling whilst interviewing him. She found it hilarious, which was a nice way of breaking the ice before the interview started. Their cat then decided that it would also have an opinion in the interview and meowed quite vocally at some points. Lesson learnt for next time: take a sandwich to eat just before I get off the train!'

The vignette above describes one researcher's awareness of herself before and during an interview with two participants. It tells us of the intrusion of her physical being into the interview, how this influenced her behaviour during the interview, how she thought she was being perceived by the participant during the interview and what she did to address that perception. In this short reflection this researcher sums up some of the key aspects researchers have to consider when they prepare for and conduct research.

In the next vignette another researcher describes some of the challenges to her role when analysing secondary data:

Researcher View

'It can feel very daunting when you start doing secondary analysis because you're aware that the data is going to be based on a different question to the one you're interested in. The data is focused on one set of questions, whilst you're focused on another so there's a kind of pressure to dig out anything relevant and a sense that you're hunting around the discussed topics to pick out the issues that weren't considered. It can get quite frustrating if the "right" questions weren't asked or potentially useful or important answers are cut short or redirected.'

This researcher highlights her awareness of examining data with questions that were not the focus of the research study. This challenge is not limited to analysis of **secondary data**; researchers analysing any data often find themselves reflecting on and asking questions of themselves about issues and topics that are not the focus of the research study. Meanings and results they find in the data may prompt new questions about the topic. Researchers can experience emotions about the topic of the study. The development of the research may provoke reminders of personal experiences. At all stages of the research process, the researcher's queries can have an effect on how the research is conducted. The development of the research question may reflect personal motivations for doing the research, the data gathering may be biased towards achieving particular results and ways in which the data is heard or tested may reflect personal and professional agendas. All forms of research take steps to recognise the researcher role, either by seeking to detach it from the research process, as when researchers are investigating objective realities, or by making it explicit as when researchers are exploring subjective realities, but as the next example shows, personal characteristics of researchers can impact research in ways that are not always manageable:

> **Researcher View**
>
> 'My job was to collect responses to a short set of questions from 200 students. To do this I was advised to approach a lecturer for permission to ask students for their participation at the end of the lecture, and to canvass for students in the main quad of the university. To me, both of these tasks represented challenges far harder than engaging them in a short survey. I am not a natural public speaker and am nervous of speaking in front of large groups. At the same time I felt unsure about approaching strangers who were having coffee or engaged in conversation in an informal communal area of the building. I think this probably showed as I only had three participants approach me at the end of the lecture and only two people agreeing to complete the survey in the quad. I was so relieved when I obtained some participants that when I administered the survey I forgot to turn over the page and so only asked half the questions.'

This researcher's nervousness overshadows both the success of recruitment and the completion of the survey, rendering the initial data unusable.

Each of these reflections highlights some of the many aspects of being a researcher. They give us a glimpse of the impact this can have on the research process and tell us that researchers are involved from the outset of the study when research questions are developed and research designs constructed, through data elicitation and gathering to data interpretation. We can believe that the data generation is influenced by the researcher even before they bring statistical tests or qualitative analysis to it. It seems obvious, too, that the ways in which a researcher chooses to present the findings, results and outcomes of their study play a key role in what is learnt by others from the research and the use and value of research.

The premise that the researcher plays a key role in all aspects of research underpins this book. The book takes as its starting point that all research involves impact by human involvement because it is conducted by humans. Whether this subjective impact is made explicit, as is common in qualitatively orientated research, or sought to be excluded, as in quantitatively orientated research, it can be placed under scrutiny by considering research in all its forms with less regard to the **methodology** brought to the research than to the researcher carrying it out. Whilst each methodology may include specific demands of researchers – to be more subjective, or more objective – this book is written in the belief that the human touch in research is present in whatever form of study is being undertaken. Ways in which this touch is made clear, obscured, removed or highlighted form the focus of discussion about practical, methodological and psychological considerations throughout. At times these are clearly delineated and affiliated to different forms of research, but as far as is possible this book aims to consider the researcher, their role, their influence and the challenges they face in ensuring high-quality credible research however they are doing it.

Why think about the researcher?

Some people will think it is not important to consider the researcher in research. Of greater importance to them may be the measurements, tests and analyses used in the research or the final outcomes of the research. Other readers may question the attention to detail being given to the researcher, and query whether this in itself will take away from the focus on the research itself. To both of these audiences this book strives to highlight that without researchers there is no research, and therefore that, without considering the researcher, a key component of the research is missing.

By reading the vignettes above you may have formed a picture of the person who wrote them. The narratives that followed the first two research vignettes indicate the sex of the researchers but little other information about them is provided. Readers may ponder what the topic of the research was, why it involved train journeys early in the morning, what data was being analysed or why the survey administrator was being instructed to recruit from student bodies. Ideas about the age, interests and experience of the researcher may have come into your mind. You may have formed opinions about the capability of each to conduct research. You may have wondered what the research was about and why the researcher was conducting it. If you were asking these questions your impression of the research itself will have been influenced. You may wonder whether the research was carried out as well as it might have been or whether the data collected was useful. If you were asking such questions you were doing so based on reading only a few lines of text. Imagine what questions you might have if you knew more about the researcher or if you were a participant engaging with research and therefore with the researchers carrying it out. However objective the research sets out to be, it is hard to imagine that these questions will not have an influence on how the research has been carried out.

This book aims to bring an awareness of what a researcher is, what that means about how research is conducted and how awareness of these concerns can increase the quality and credibility of research practice. After reading it you will be equipped with tips and strategies, as well as information and (hopefully) more questions about how to consider yourself in your research. If inserting yourself as a researcher in your research comes to mean that you need to find ways of recognising objectivity and subjectivity and of working to adjust these to the benefit of the research, then the book will have achieved one of its purposes. If the practical and psychological challenges of working as a lone researcher or as one of a team become clearer, and you are equipped with ways of addressing them as a result of reading this book, then a key aim of the book will have been achieved. If you did not realise how important you are to the research prior to reading this book then it will have gone a long way to enhancing your research career and the quality of your research.

Who is 'the researcher'?

In the broadest possible sense everyone who is human is a researcher. As we go about our daily lives we continually form and test hypotheses about other people, about events and experiences, and about our own behaviour and choices. We make predictions about what we expect to happen and test them out through our experiences and observations. We form new questions and ideas when we encounter realities that conform or otherwise, and we seek information from others about issues of interest and concern to us. In everyday life our informal research practice enables us to learn, anticipate, react, develop and revise understandings of ourselves, the world around us and our interactions with and within it. As a formal researcher conducting research within academic or professional contexts the researcher is anyone who is involved with the devising, conducting and reporting of the research. Sometimes this is one person throughout, other times there may be different researchers involved in different aspects of the research process. As an informal researcher only the outcomes of the research may be of primary importance to you but as a formal researcher the outcomes are shared with others to bring them new insights, enable them to ask new questions and to understand and improve practice, often with the aim of bringing about change. This makes it of paramount importance that every possible step is taken throughout the research process to ensure that the research is carried out in trustworthy and appropriate ways that consider all the influences that can have an impact.

To ensure that such research is truly useful and can be relied upon by others, models and tests of analysis have been devised to be used within frameworks of ontological, epistemological and theoretical underpinnings. It is the formal researcher's role to select the frameworks and methods they are going to use to make inquiry into research questions and hypotheses, and it is their role to design, carry out and report the research to the interested audiences. It is at these intersections of decision-making, conduct and presentation with and of research that this book considers the researcher. Who is the person making and enacting these choices and what is their impact on the research?

Reflective Question: People, places, events, experiences.
What are the sorts of things that you research in your everyday life using expectations, predictions, curiosity and hunches?

In formal research two dominant approaches to the methodology employed are used: **quantitative research** approaches, that measure, test and hypothesise, and **qualitative research** approaches, that ask questions, seek descriptions and look for meanings. Each approach asks different questions through research and seeks different types of knowledge from it. Each has its own philosophical underpinnings, techniques and forms of analysis. A key difference between them is how the researcher is regarded and the next sections considers this.

A NOTE ON TERMINOLOGY

The division between different approaches to research, in which references are often made to 'qualitative' or 'quantitative' research, has led to a rhetoric that risks categorising researchers similarly. Assumptions about the world view taken by researchers are commonly associated with the two different paradigms. This means that qualitative researchers are widely regarded as seeing the world as constructed, and quantitative researchers as seeing the world as being of fixed realities to be discovered. These assumptions inherently place the researchers within or outside the research and do not easily allow for 'quantitative' researchers who hold the view that theories applied to research data are themselves social constructions (such as views of sexual development based only on behaviour) or for 'qualitative' researchers who hold the view that the realities of the world can be imperfectly constructed (such as views of medical care based only on biological evidence). In order to broaden the discussions in this book about the role of the researcher in all forms of research I seek to avoid such categorisations by referring to researchers who are 'subjective' (placing themselves and what they bring to the research within the research practice) or 'objective' (seeking to detach themselves from the research process) regardless of an apparent alignment to a qualitative or quantitative paradigm. It is true that often subjective researchers employ qualitative methods and that objective researchers commonly are those employing quantitative methods, but this is not always the case. To enable readers to think widely about what it is about researchers that is important and relevant to research practice, I use the terms **subjective researcher** and **objective researcher** throughout the book.

The objective researcher

Objective researchers assume that an independent reality exists outside of any investigation or observation, and the role of research is to uncover this reality. In order to detach themselves from the research, objective researchers employ a range of techniques. They adopt a neutral stance to the research by, for example, remaining separate from the participants when they are completing tests, seeking triangulation of results using other tests and employing inter-rater reliability strategies so that results reached by other researchers can be used in comparison with those reached in their own study.

Quantitative research can be understood as research that systematically investigates and measures observable phenomena. It is usually predicated on the existence of a universal truth that the researcher sets out to test through hypotheses and experiments that aim to be **generalisable, valid, robust** and **reliable**. The researcher is regarded as a **confounding variable** that the research is designed to exclude so that the results of the study can be regarded as applicable and repeatable regardless of who is administering the tests in future projects. Whilst the results of some objective studies may be questioned, the role of the researcher is rarely considered, because they are not seen as being part of the research itself. However, researchers can have an impact in several ways.

Partington (2009) identifies three aspects of the individual that can influence the research: personal interest and perspective, personal relationship to the data and personal characteristics. Personal interest is often behind decisions about what to research. Whether this is based on experiences, observations of others, professional practice or a desire to address an issue that has been concerning the researcher, it has an effect on what research questions are asked, how they are asked and in what context. Personal relationships with the data influence how data is collected and from whom. Researchers' involvement with the topic and the ways they understand those who are contributing data can impact on what data is elicited and what responses participants choose to give. These issues also affect what questions the researcher asks of the data, how they test it and what meanings they bring to its interpretations. Personal characteristics of a researcher can influence the research design and strategies as well as their administration of the research. If a researcher is more comfortable working with pen and paper than in speaking with people they may use computer-based tests rather than face-to-face questionnaires, for example, therefore devising the study in ways that limit the hypotheses that can be tested.

Reflective Question: If you are thinking about something can you be objective in your understanding of it?

A well-known example of a study in psychology to test responses to authority figures helps to illustrate some of these points.

RESEARCH EXAMPLE

Research summary from Milgram, S. (1963). Behavioral study of obedience. *Journal of Abnormal and Social Psychology, 67*(4), 371–378.

This study was conducted by a social psychologist, Stanley Milgram, in 1961. It was devised shortly after the first televised screening of the trial of a Nazi war criminal. Milgram was born to a Jewish family in New York City, the child of a Romanian-born mother and Hungarian-born father. The study he devised aimed to test whether people will simply 'follow orders' as was argued by some of the war criminals on trial at the time. He recruited and paid 40 Yale University students, who volunteered to take part in a study that he said was about memory and learning. By asking the students to pick slips of paper apparently at random, the study was engineered so that each participant became a 'Teacher' to an unseen 'Learner' who was in an adjacent room. The Learner was in fact an actor recruited for the role in the study. The Teacher was told that their job was to teach the Learner specified word pairs. Teachers were told that the Learner was wired up to a machine that was capable of giving electric shocks. The strength of the shocks could be increased at the Teacher's discretion using switches and levers. The researcher (the 'Experimenter') stayed in the room with the Teacher and gave instructions (pre-decided) on when and why to continue administering shocks when Learner responses were given. The results of the study showed that 65 per cent of the Teachers continued to administer shocks on the instructions of the Experimenter, even when they heard screams and pleas for help coming from the adjacent room, and in spite of also having been told that the Learner had a potentially dangerous heart condition, to which the Learner referred when the level of the shocks increased.

This study and its findings, whilst criticised for its lack of ethical consideration (many of the Teachers were left traumatised by their involvement in the study), was widely hailed as proving that human beings will show obedience to authority by shifting responsibility for their actions to others. It appeared to explain the rise and behaviour of Naziism and Nazis, and was used in many other areas of human behaviour enquiry including military training and behaviour.

The study has since been questioned and critiqued with arguments that the results were not reported in full. Perry (2014) reports that the 65 per cent obedience statistic has been wrongly conflated from a series of 24 experimental trials, each with different variations, scripts, actors and experimental set-ups. She found that across the trials, 60 per cent of participants disobeyed the instructions given by the researcher. The fact that the experiment involved only 40 subjects is often overlooked in reporting this study, and that there was variation in conditions across the trials and the participants.

When considering this study in relation to being an objective researcher, it is useful to think about Milgram the person, and the zeitgeist of the times. Milgram's personal interest and perspective on Nazi war crimes is likely to have been evoked by his personal heritage and by the prevailing international context in which Holocaust survivors were shown on television giving witness to unthinkable behaviours. Those accused of carrying out the behaviours often appeared impassive and ordinary as they stood in the dock. Milgram's relationship to the data can be understood to have arisen from his recent appointment to Yale a year previously, and his desire to make his mark as a researcher. His PhD had been conducted under the supervision of Solomon Asch, a prominent Gestalt psychologist and a pioneer of social psychology. The PhD extended Asch's work on conformity, whilst also no doubt planting the seed of interest in this area for Milgram who extended it by considering differences across two cultures for his PhD thesis. Milgram may have been keen to be seen to be independent of Asch and able to conduct ground-breaking research himself so that he could establish his credentials as an independent researcher. The study itself was designed over the course of almost a year, using Milgram's Psychology of the Small Group class to rehearse it with students to enable them to acquire skills considered useful to social psychology research: story-telling, acting and stagecraft. Milgram's personal characteristics can be gleaned from sources (e.g. Blass, 2004; Perry, 2014) that describe him as having a wide range of interests that included drama, paint-ing, debating and international relations. He was initially rejected from joining Harvard's Department of Social Relations to pursue his PhD, and spent a year taking graduate courses in psychology to ensure success on a second application. On completion of his PhD he moved to Yale and started to apply for funding to conduct new experiments to test obedience. After a number of rejections of the grant applications, a proposal was eventually approved by the National Science Foundation. Interestingly, given the level of controversy that his study provoked, Milgram is reported to have been unusual for the time, in debriefing participants to ensure their well-being after taking part in studies and asking them for their thoughts on the ethics of various studies. On a personal level he met his wife-to-be in his first year at Yale, and both went on to become politically active, contacting local politicians and writing letters to university newspapers. He was reportedly a dedicated father, playing games and talking with his children whilst taking many trips with them (Psyography, 2015).

From this brief outline we can make some assumptions that Milgram was determined about pursuing his research interest in conformity, cultural differences and obedience. We can ponder that the long strug-gle in having his proposal accepted led to a greater desire to see the study through. His perspective on the behaviour of those who commit evil acts may have been a fixed positivist one and he may have had a political desire to publicise explanations and descriptions of acts car-ried out in the name of obedience.

We cannot know how all of this impacted on the research he con-ducted and reported but we can infer Milgram was the key person behind the idea, the design, the conduct and the reporting of the famous study. Without him it may not have happened and whilst the reliability of it is now being questioned and further explored, it is also true that at the time the results, although controversial, were accepted, widely disseminated and used as a platform for a huge range of new studies and research directions. For researchers, this raises questions about motivation, agenda, purpose and reporting of research they conduct, and the responsibility invested in them for doing so.

The subjective researcher

In contrast to the researcher who seeks to remain neutral and objective in the research process, subjective researchers start from the assumption that their presence and involvement in the research has an effect and elicits data that is likely to be more representative of the complexities of human experience and interaction. Subjective researchers employ quality criteria such as **transparency, trustworthiness** and **reflexivity** to make their involvement in the research process as explicit as possible. In practice this means that they consider what assumptions and biases they are bringing to the research and how these inform the research questions they develop, the methods for eliciting data from participants, their selection of data for analysis, and the interrogation and interpretation of the data. Subjective researchers do this by keeping reflexive journals in which they record thoughts, ideas, reflections and questions arising from their experience of the research. They may also employ more than one technique for finding meanings in data so that the assumptions of different methods and their use are brought together to view the data more holistically and with less imposition of one researcher or method (e.g. Frost et al., 2010). Interpretations may be discussed with other researchers and supervisors to gain more understanding of subjective influences. Subjective researchers commonly employ qualitative approaches to their research to seek out meanings and descriptions brought by different individuals and groups to experiences and events.

Subjective researchers start from the premise that human behaviour is context-dependent. Context may range from the historical, cultural and political histories of participants and groups to the setting for the data collection itself. The subjective researcher positions themselves within the research process, rather than outside it as an objective researcher strives to do, and regards the research as co-constructed between the participants and themselves. They recognise that there are inherent power dynamics between the researcher and the researched, and strive to flatten this hierarchy through processes of self-awareness, interactions with participants and openness in the conduct and reporting of research.

Many of the considerations of the role of subjectivity in research have come from **feminist research**. This approach emerged in the UK and the US in the 1960s, and considers both the focus of the research and the researcher's role in carrying it out.

Feminist research

Developed in response to the perception of male bias in published research, feminist research sought to introduce women's perspectives by including women in the research process to correct and challenge such biases. Arguably pioneered by Carol Gilligan's 1977 study of moral development – later published as a book, *In a Different Voice* (1982) – the problems with the tradition of psychological research that treated women as if they were men began to be highlighted. The book focused on moral development and found that gender differences played an important role. Crucially, however, Gilligan pointed out that rather than there being something wrong with women for not developing in the same way as men, there must instead be something wrong with a theory that suggests that they do.

Critiques of positivism and objectivity that positioned women outside research or grouped them with men, with no regard to differences arising from sex or gender, led to the central principle of objectivity being converted into 'feminist objectivity'. Feminist objectivity frames concepts such as knowledge and truth as always being partial and inseparable from the experiences of the researched. Considering this as 'situated knowledge' Haraway (1988) argues that knowledge and truth are always subjective, power-imbued and relational. This was illustrated in Gilligan's findings that women had been found to reach a lower level of moral development in previous studies because the participants were largely men and the scoring method used a way of reasoning that was more favourable to boys than the moral argumentation that concentrates on relations and is more favoured by girls.

Through a further turn that recognised that women are not only different to men but also to each other, feminist research provoked techniques and methods that enable questions about who has access to knowledge and whose knowledge is accessed to be asked and addressed. Feminist researchers interrogate the data through lenses that consider intersections of gender with personal dimensions such as class, race, age, ability, sexuality and so on, and critique taken-for-granted assumptions about women's experiences. Feminist researchers therefore seek to inquire into individual meaning-making in ways that provide a range of methods for participants to express themselves and which are employed with the explicit inclusion of the researcher as part of the process. Understanding of women's experiences is developed in conjunction with women themselves, so enabling individuals and groups who are at risk of being marginalised or obscured in research to be acknowledged and heard. The research is carried out *with* the researched instead of *about* them and although commonly adopts an interpretivist stance, also allows for feminist researchers who hold realist or critical realist world views (see later in this chapter for more on Epistemology).

The subjective researcher that has evolved from the development of feminist research can use themselves both to inform the research and to be aware of impositions they are at risk of bringing to it. One example of how this works in practice can be seen in research about motherhood, conducted by women who are mothers themselves.

RESEARCH EXAMPLE

Research summary from Frost, N. A. (2009). Do you know what I mean?: The use of a pluralistic narrative analysis interpretation of an interview. *Qualitative Research, 9*(1), 9–29.

This study aimed to explore the experience of women making the transition from being the mother of one child to becoming a mother of two children. Seven women were recruited for a series of semi-structured interviews with the researcher that began when the mother was six months pregnant with her second child and ended when the child was nine months old. The researcher was a recent mother to a second child and employed different models of narrative analysis to elicit and analyse accounts from women about issues and experiences of significance to them over the year-long period of the study. Findings from the interview included that the mothers sought to use the experience of having a second child to plan for the birth to be a different (better) experience than that of their first child, that they were concerned about how they would retain the intensity of the relationship with their first child once the second child was born, and that once the second child was born they wanted to be alone with the child for the first few months, sometimes regarding the first child as a troublemaker or danger to the baby.

The researcher found that once she had told the mothers that she was also a second-time mother, the language they used and the stories they told were different to those they had used and told before this had been disclosed. Phrases such as '*you know what I mean*' implied assumed shared knowledge; participants started speaking in terms of '*we*', referring to the researcher and herself, rather than '*I*' when talking about activities with the children; and difficulties of combining paid employment with children were described. When gathering the data the researcher found herself sometimes challenged by mother–baby interactions that were different to her own, such as a crying baby not being attended to by the mother,

(Continued)

believing that she would not leave her own child alone when it was crying. In the interpretation of the data the researcher's awareness of her presence as a mother and as a researcher meant that she attended more to the unspoken content of the accounts, such as the implications of a perceived or imposed lack of choice in providing care to children at the expense of other responsibilities, and the use of metaphors to describe emotions that could not be named. She was better able to recognise when she had closed down conversations that were uncomfortable for her. The analysis of the data and a summary of the findings were provided to each participant at the conclusion of the study so that participants had the opportunity to discuss the interpretations the researcher had brought to their accounts of this transition period of their lives.

The subjective and objective researcher

Researchers who use both quantitative and qualitative methods in their research studies have to consider their subjectivity and objectivity in light of using methods that may require them to be both part of the research and detached from it. As has been discussed above, subjectivity can play a role in both. Qualitative research generally promotes a subjective stance and requires researchers not only to consider themselves in the research process but also to make this explicit. Quantitative research promotes an objective stance and does not provide space for subjective influence in either its conduct or its reporting. The challenge for researchers using mixed-methods approaches can therefore be how to position themselves and their view of the knowledge they are seeking, and how to use and present this in the research they carry out. Hesse-Biber (2010) and others have argued that by ensuring that methods are selected and used as tools best suited for the pursuit of knowledge appropriate to the research question, researchers can keep awareness of themselves central to all aspects of the research. Even this can be challenging when a researcher who is schooled in one research approach or another, as is often the case, is required to broaden their view of the part they play in research. Bryman (2007) has pointed out that challenges can arise from mixed-methods researchers being more skilled or biased towards a particular approach and regarding the other as less important to the research. Such bias can lead to findings made using one approach being overlooked or downplayed in the development of the research, and not reported in its final outcomes. Forming a team of researchers may be seen to be one way of addressing this but this, too, can lead to challenges in reaching ways of deciding the status of each method and of valuing it, and the researcher who uses it.

Qualitatively driven mixed-methods research (e.g. Hesse-Biber, 2010; Mason, 2006) places researcher subjectivity at the centre of mixed-methods research whilst also recognising the contribution of objectively reached findings. Qualitatively driven mixed-methods research is conducted by considering three levels of mixing in the research process: at the data-gathering stage, at the data-analysis stage and at the data-interpretation stage. Mixing at the data-gathering stage allows a subset of participants from a large sample gathered for a quantitative method, such as a survey, to be selected for a subsequent qualitative study in order to extend the generalisation of the findings from the qualitative study to a wider population. It can also define a population of interest within a larger quantitative study that had not been anticipated at the outset of the research or to identify a representative sample. The researcher is aware of the purpose of the method and recognises their motivation and agenda for using it. Mixing at the data-analysis stage seeks to highlight results and findings that are contradictory or divergent, as well as those that converge. By integrating the findings of each method in the pursuit of one overarching research question, differences between the two can be transcended and both can be considered alongside each other to develop a richer and multi-layered view of the same topic of interest. Throughout, the researcher is aware of what knowledge they are seeking through the process, how it is relevant to the research question and the differing impacts of their role in each phase.

Using qualitative approaches as the driver of mixed-methods research allows new empirical and theoretical perspectives to be brought to the study design, both by uncovering new insights using in-depth qualitative methods and by considering the researcher subjectivity throughout the process. It asks not only what knowledge has been acquired but also by whom. It centres the lived experience of the participants, as constructed with the researcher, in the research and seeks to uncover subjugated knowledge not otherwise accessible by considering who is seeking the knowledge and how it has been generated. Conflict between the methods is minimal as both play a role in either generalising, confirming, extending or detailing the research at the levels of data-collection analysis or interpretation. A sound theoretical foundation is established by maintaining the research question as the focus of the research and all that is carried out during it. Thus the qualitatively driven mixed-methods approach allows research to move beyond the simply qualitative, subjectively influenced perspective to be brought to the addressing of the research problem to provide mixed-method explanations of research questions.

The team-based researcher

The team-based researcher works alongside researchers with different skills and theoretical orientations to explore the same topic. Many team researchers highlight the importance of communication when working as part of a team; some incorporate dialogic analysis and interpretation into the research as an additional resource (e.g. Katsiaficas, Futch, Fine, & Sirin, 2011). Mason (2006) highlights the usefulness of the possibility of 'dialogic explanations'. Dialogic explanations arise from the exchange of ideas (Sullivan, 2012) and so, can enable multiple questions, meanings and relevancies 'to be held together in creative tension and dynamic relation within the explanation itself' (Mason, 2006, p. 20). Different perspectives, which may be a selection of abstract ideas gained from professional, research-based or theoretical knowledge, understandings gained through personal experience, and/or personal values and judgements, are brought to the explanation. As the following moving quote from a mother who lost both her children in the Air India Flight 182 bomb attack of 1985 off the coast of south-west Ireland shows, dialogic explanations can be brought by one person who includes ideas as lived (Bakhtin, 1981) as well as ideas as concepts:

> As a scientist I knew at once no-one could have survived. But as a mother it is different. Until recently that part of me would come to Ireland each year thinking, 'Well maybe there will be a miracle and the boys will return'. (Padmini Turlapati quoted in BBC News (Dowd, 2015).)

Dialogic explanations in research allow for different understandings to be brought by methods and by researchers, and for the different interrelationships between them to be incorporated. When working as part of a team this can be challenging as well as productive, as agreements, disagreements and debates take place. At a practical level it is an important way to establish roles and allow for different researcher input, as is expressed in the following Researcher View:

Researcher View

'So I know that we have to get kind of clear in advance what people's roles are and who's going to do what and all that sort of thing.... I think we did have regular meetings to try and make sure that everything was, you know, happening as it was supposed to.'

The importance of these meetings, though, also lies in developing efficient communication at them and in managing the tasks that arise from them:

Researcher View

'So the challenges were trying to keep up that communication and then, like I said, when the funded project ended, the communications sort of fell away a bit because for them it was over, then they had written their report for the funder and that was it. But obviously for us one of our objectives was to get stuff published in the public domain.'

When efficient communication is established, dialogues about the research process can take place. Reflecting on the role of communication amongst researchers, one researcher said:

Researcher View

'I guess it's about trying to keep in mind what the goal of the research is going to be as a health psychologist.... I worked actually in a, well, it was an interdisciplinary team but they were all academics working with an external organisation. So I was working with a psychologist and a sociologist who was specialising in social policy.... I found that I had overlapping things in common with each of them.'

The value of finding overlaps and commonalities can be in seeking out common understandings of the research goals whilst also understanding the perspective brought by other team members. This enables dialogic explanations to be constructed in which multiple perspectives can lead to new insight and understanding.

Communication amongst team members can be developed to become a useful addition to the repertoire of tools that the team can offer, by addressing, querying and working with difference as well as with commonalities. Questioning a researcher about the research question they are bringing to the research not only can help to clarify perspectives for the questioner but also encourages the questioned researcher to consider carefully why they are asking the question and what its value to the research project is. Such dialogue can only be carried out in conditions that feel safe to all team members in order to reduce the risk of individuals feeling criticised or undervalued (see Chapter 4 for more on this).

Consideration of and communication about what questions are being asked of the data, why these questions have been devised and the theoretical orientations underlying them, makes space for the personal, theoretical and empirical influences in the research process.

Reflective Question: What is the hardest question you could be asked about your research? Is it about your personal interest in the topic? The approach you have taken to it? Or the findings you have reached?

The dialogic explanation approach is well suited to interdisciplinary and team-based mixed-methods research, and allows for different skill sets and beliefs to be brought together in creative dialogue. The responsibility for the richness of the dialogue and the related outcomes of the quality and scope of the explanation lies with each team member and how they transcend differences between them to work together as mixed-methods researchers. However, it is not only personal characteristics that are brought to research. How researchers understand and make sense of the world and what they regard as underlying these processes are also key to their subjective view of it, and are important underpinnings of research approaches. Together with methodology, **ontology** and **epistemology** form research **paradigms** within which research is conducted.

Ontology

Ontology is formed of the beliefs and assumptions that individuals hold about what exists in the world. It defines for them what is real, how things really are and how things really work (Lincoln & Denzin, 1998). This can be understood using the 'allegory of the cave', a tale allegedly recited by Plato and included in *Republic* (Plato, 2008). Plato describes a group of prisoners kept in a cave since childhood, always bound by the neck and hands so that they cannot turn their heads. The light of the sunshine at the opening to the cave behind them and from a fire on a raised parapet above and behind them enables shadows of objects carried on their jailers' heads as they walk along to be cast on the wall that is all the prisoners can look upon. Knowing nothing else, the prisoners assume the shadows to be objects themselves and label them according to what they see and how the jailers talk about them. Imagining that one prisoner is eventually released Plato describes their gradual ascent out of the cave into the sunlight when with an adjustment to the new and bright context the former prisoner comes to realise that all that they had seen before were only shadows. If this prisoner were to return to the cave to share this insight with the other prisoners, they would likely find themselves ridiculed and labelled as deranged. On their part they would be dismissive and pitying of the prisoners' beliefs that what they are seeing (the shadows) are what is real. Plato's tale is understood to represent the need not to rely only on sensory perceptions to understand the world and instead to use the light of philosophy (the sun) to bring intellectual meaning to it. The mutual derision between former prisoner and current prisoner is argued to represent the lack of desire of humans to seek out meanings based on clear philosophical and intellectual underpinnings.

In contemporary research a number of ontological assumptions are brought to research practice based on what researchers regard as 'real' in the world. Researchers with a **realism** ontology believe there is an objective reality that can be identified, tested and understood through the laws that govern it. Researchers with a **critical realism** ontology believe that there is independent reality but that observation is fallible and therefore the ability to know reality with certainty is questionable. Researchers with a **constructivist** ontology believe that reality is constructed through dissemination of assumptions and discourses. **Social constructionists** believe that reality is created through interaction with the social world we inhabit. In research terms, constructionist and social constructionist ontologies place a great emphasis on the role of language in creating realities, and realism and critical realism ontologies maintain that reality exists to be uncovered regardless of social structures.

RESEARCH EXAMPLE

Summary of research from Steffen, E., & Coyle, A. (2015). 'I thought they should know ... that daddy is not completely gone': A case study of sense-of-presence experiences in bereavement and family meaning-making, *Omega: Journal of Death and Dying*.

The study: This research explores the meaning-making brought by one family to the experiences of sensing the presence of the deceased father, and the relation of the meaning-making to spiritual understanding. By employing a pluralistic qualitative approach that brings both phenomenological and social constructionist inquiry to the discursive and thematic analysis of the interviews and to the observations of the family as a whole, of

(Continued)

individual members, and to meaningful events associated with the deceased father, the researchers ask:

What role, if any, might sense-of-presence experiences play in a bereaved family?
How do members of a family experience and make (shared) sense of this phenomenon?
What relationship, if any, might there be between such experiences and family members' belief systems?
What are the personal and social implications of disclosing the experience?
How is the experience perceived to impact, if at all, on the family as a whole?

The participants: A family that had been bereaved for at least 18 months and in which at least one family member reported at least one sense-of-presence experience was recruited. The family consisted of a mother and three children aged 16 (a daughter), 14 and 12 (two sons). The family had lived in England for four and a half years, having come from a Central European country. The father died relatively shortly after they arrived, unexpectedly and from an undiagnosed health problem that could have been treated if it had been detected. Family members described themselves as Roman Catholic, with the mother rating religion and/or spirituality as 'extremely' important in her life, the daughter and the 14-year-old son rating it as 'quite' important and the 12-year-old rating religion and/or spirituality as 'not very' important.

Data collection: A semi-structured interview was held with the whole family to explore the felt absence/presence of the deceased, the meaning of the sense-of-presence experiences of the family as a whole and individually, the relationship of the experiences with the family belief systems, and the significance of sharing the experiences. This was followed by three participant observations of experiences that the family perceived as being connected to the father. These were attending church, playing Cluedo and visiting a historical site that had been special to the father. Field notes were made by the researchers and subsequently shared with the family for comments. Comment and feedback were explored in a second family interview. Finally, each family member was offered the opportunity to have an individual interview, an opportunity taken up by the mother and the daughter.

Data analysis: The specific lifeworld of the participants' perspectives was analysed through the observation data by adopting a phenomenological stance that sought to gain insight into the naturalistic settings of the participants. Discursive aspects of the interview data, such as the establishment of credible accounts and warding off of alternative interpretations, were analysed using a social constructionist stance. Several readings of the field notes were made in order to contextualise the findings but were kept separate from the overall analysis, in recognition of their constitution of the realities seen through the fieldworker's eyes rather than those of the participants.

Findings: The phenomenologically orientated analysis of the interview data produced three overarching themes, each with subthemes:

- Making sense of sense of presence
  - Sense of presence of veridical events (Mother)
  - Sense of presence requiring scientific explanation (Children)
- Individual meanings of sense of presence experiences
  - Sense of presence as beneficial (Mother)
    - Sense of presence as comforting
    - Sense of presence as confirming the continuing bond
    - Sense of presence as strengthening beliefs
  - Sense of presence as disturbing (Children)
    - Sense of presence as dissonant
    - Sense of presence as uncomfortable
    - Need for certainty
- Perceived impact of sense of presence on the family (Family)
  - Sense of presence as conveying the father's continued participation in family life (Mother)
  - Sense of presence as concerning the perceiver (Children)
  - Lack of impact of sense of presence on the family as a whole (Children)

The discursive perspective provided a micro-level insight into how meanings were negotiated by the family. The mother was described as 'claiming objectivity of sense of presence' through normalising and first-hand witnessing accounts. By contrast the children positioned themselves as 'dismissing sense of presence experiences' by drawing on scientific discourses, discounting their mother's evidence and challenging her credibility.

The observational data highlighted the division between the mother and the children's meaning-making, for example in the theme 'Challenges to the mother's parental authority'.

Discussion: The study highlights the multiple ontologies of what is real to each member of the family, as well as how the family as a whole strives to make meaning of the phenomenon. The world views of the children can be seen to reject the mother's interpretations, and also to bring wider family dynamics to the fore. The ways in which they seek to add weight to their rejection of the mother's interpretations can be seen in their use of culturally dominant explanatory frameworks framed within scientific paradigms seeking evidence and falsification. The mother's veridical 'felt' experiences of the presence of the deceased father can be understood to be closer to a minority family culture of emotional expressiveness, and linked to the mother's spiritual beliefs about the afterlife, whilst the children's dismissal of her interpretations can be understood to have arisen from the dissonance with their world views of needing scientifically explainable phenomena.

(Continued)

Implications: What is perceived to be real to members of this family has been shown to differ, and the ways that they make meaning of the phenomenon draw on different underlying frameworks of spiritual beliefs and scientifically based understandings. The multiple ontologies highlighted by this family have important implications for the development of therapeutic practice with bereaved families, which should consider not only the complexity of issues that can exist for each member but also the systemic impact of other members' experiencing and reporting sense-of-presence experiences.

Epistemology

Epistemology is the study of knowledge and how it is produced. It considers questions of what knowledge is, how it is acquired, and for feminist researchers, who has access to it. It raises issues about what is regarded as truth, presented as truth and by whom. A researcher with a realism ontology will use language to access truth; a researcher with a constructivist ontology will regard language as constituting truth, talking ideas and practices into being. Epistemological assumptions influence how researchers define their roles, what they consider ethical practice and the relationship between them and their participants (Hesse-Biber, 2014). The epistemological stance that a researcher employs will determine the methods they bring to the research and the ways in which they use those methods.

The following research example, taken from a wider paper, queries evidence-based clinical practice that targets self-harming behaviour to highlight different understandings and implications of knowledge between service users, researchers and service providers.

RESEARCH EXAMPLE

Summary of research from Warner, A., & Spandler, H. (2012). **New strategies for practice-based evidence: A focus on self-harm.** *Qualitative Research in Psychology, 9,* **13–26.**

The study: The study uses the concept of 'self-harm' to argue that research should be informed by effective principles for practice that incorporate service users' values and aspirations to provide more holistic and contextual understandings of clinical practice. This is in contrast to the existing focus on assessment of particular intervention techniques that primarily use structured and behavioural-based outcome measures.

A problem with current research identified: The priority given to large-scale outcome or prevalence studies can obscure classification and complexity of concepts such as 'self-harm' because they rarely explore intent and meaning. Qualitative research (e.g. Spandler, 1996) has shown that self-harm serves various functions for service users, and that the meaning of experiences is complex and shifting. Service development recommendations are often based on a main outcome measure of suicidal behaviour, an outcome that only represents the potential relationships between self-harm and suicidal behaviour.

The argument: Mental distress such as that associated with self-harm arises from negative, oppressive or abusive experiences in the social world (Scottish Development Centre, 2005) which individuals experience differently therefore recognising the meaning that each person gives to the behaviour is likely to differ. Self-harm can be a coping strategy and/or a means of ending life and can have positive and negative effects within and between different people at different times (Spandler, 1996).

Conclusion: The focus of 'stopping' self-harming behaviour should not be at the expense of other considerations that are important to the service user. The researchers call for monitoring of services that is focused on service users, and allows for changing and differing meanings of the behaviour to those carrying it out.

The combination of ontology and epistemology with methodology (the tools selected to work within the epistemological and ontological framework) forms research paradigms – 'the set of common beliefs and arguments shared between scientists about how problems should be understood and addressed' (Kuhn, 1962). Common paradigms are **positivism** (realism ontology, in which truth is independent of social structures), **post positivism** (critical realism ontology in which context is regarded as necessary to gain understanding), and **interpretivism** (constructionist or social constructionist ontology in which many truths exist and arise through language and interaction). For the researcher the question in all of these is the value of their presence in obtaining sound research results, and this can be considered through reflexive processes.

Reflexivity

Reflexivity is an umbrella term for practices that allow the researcher to explore their impact on the research they are conducting. It is a quality criterion for qualitative research but has relevance for all forms of research. Reflexivity can take many forms, and focuses on the personal, methodological and epistemological stances that researchers bring to the research. By reflecting on their relationship with the research, researchers are able to consider in detail the decisions they are making about its conduct and the tools with which they are carrying it out. Researchers develop an awareness of the assumptions and biases they are bringing to the study and can choose how to use or reduce these in research practice. They can make explicit what impact they are aware of having on the research, and find ways to understand the data generated by the context in which the research was done and how that may have influenced the knowledge that it produced. Reflexive consideration of context can extend beyond the research setting itself, from the historical situatedness of the participants and the research topic through to the prevailing norms and discourses that form part of the research.

There is no one way to be reflexive in research, and indeed there are many different forms of reflexivity. Finlay (2003) has identified five forms of reflexivity:

FINLAY'S FIVE FORMS OF REFLEXIVITY

Reflexivity as introspection: the researcher considers their own experience and uses it to understand the experience of others. The link between knowledge claims, personal experience and the experience of others is made as explicit as possible.

Reflexivity as intersubjective reflection: exploration of the research relationship in order to gain insight into the meanings created and/or mutually understood within it.

Reflexivity as mutual collaboration: researchers as participants and participants as researchers in the adoption of a co-operative inquiry stance.

Reflexivity as social critique: the use of reflexivity to seek ways to address power imbalances in the research process, for example by making explicit issues of class, gender and ethnicity.

Reflexivity as ironic deconstruction: seeks to make multiple voices heard by challenging the rhetoric of a 'voice of authority' within the research process.

For more detail, see: Finlay, L. (2003). The reflexive journey: mapping multiple routes. In L. Finlay & B. Gough (Eds). *Reflexivity: A practical guide for researchers in health and social sciences*. Oxford: Blackwell Publishing.

Wilkinson (1988) identified three approaches to reflexive practice. The 'personal approach' seeks to highlight individual characteristics that the researcher may bring to the research. These may include motivation for carrying out the research, personal attitudes to the topic under study and intended applications of the research outcomes. The 'functional approach' considers the role of the researcher and the impact of this on the process. This may be about understanding the different identities that the researcher adopts during the process (such as 'expert', 'inquirer', 'collaborator', 'author'), and how these affect the balance of power at different points in the process. The 'disciplinary approach' adopts a critical perspective on the research in order to illuminate conflicts and debates between theory and method, and often, to challenge existing research findings.

Reflexive practice therefore ranges from the purely 'confessional' to considering its co-constructedness and socially situatedness. Challenges for the researcher are not only to develop personal insight into how they are conducting research but also to avoid imposing their own story on to that of the participant and risking being narcissistic and overindulgent in the consideration of personal reactions and emotions (Gough, 2003).

In order to be reflexive, researchers maintain reflexive journals, seek peer support for reflexive dialogue and use supervision processes to raise questions and highlight concerns. Despite this, researchers cannot expect to be fully aware of all that they bring to research. Unconscious motivations and influences will not be known to them, nor the way that they are perceived by participants. Reflexivity in research practice, however, enables subjective involvement in research that allows examination of personal experiences, pre-existing knowledge and understandings in ways that help to develop more thoughtful, conceptual analysis and interpretation. Whether this is made explicit or not may depend on the expectations of the research paradigm in which the research is being conducted.

This chapter has shown how a researcher can be subjective and/or objective by considering their ontological, epistemological and methodological positions in relation to the research question(s). Reflexivity provides ways in which they can consider their stance in relation to their involvement in the research, the choice and employment of methods they use, and an adherence to a clear view of what knowledge they are seeking to test or acquire through the research question. These concepts are valuable to researchers considering their role in research when they are researching from within one, or across more than one, paradigm. An additional layer to these considerations is that of ethics. Ethical stances adopted by researchers are closely related to their subjective positioning, and how they regard the research topic, the involvement of participants and the value of the research.

The ethical researcher

All research requires ethical consideration, and most is carried out under Ethical Guidelines of research institutions and discipline- and practice-specific governing bodies. Guidelines typically require researchers to take all possible precautions to ensure confidentiality and anonymity, to minimise distress to participants during and after their participation in the study – see for example the *Code of Ethics and Conduct* (British Psychological Society, 2009) and the *Code of Human Research Ethics* (British Psychological Society, 2010) – and for the researcher to take self-care precautions. **Positive ethics** can also be brought to the inquiry by researchers.

A positive ethical stance advocates that researchers consider their actions in the promotion of the good of the individual and the com- munity of which they are a part (Knapp & Van de Creek, 2006). In practice this can include providing participants with opportunities to contribute to research about an issue that is of importance to them, or to one not previously researched, taking responsibility for eliciting and presenting data in a way that is morally and ethically justifiable (such as by creating a safe environment in which participants feel they can talk openly to researchers), and by considering how as a researcher the accounts and other expressions of experience are being listened to, heard and interpreted. When presenting research for a wider audience, researchers can consider how they are respecting not only what has been told to them but also how it is told to the wider world by writing in an accessible style that stays true to the original data. It is also important for researchers to take extra caution when reporting on what has not been said or when drawing on theories that allude to the unconscious or other abstract concepts to enrich data.

The following extract from a researcher's reflexive journal illus- trates some of the issues arising for researchers when seeking to bring a positive ethical stance to research.

REFLECTIVE JOURNAL EXTRACT

I can use my own experience of being a mother as an example of the way in which I retained awareness of this ethical responsibility. The mundane and repetitive tasks of childcare and day-to-day living with two children were not directly spoken of in the interviews and I wonder if they were consid- ered by the participants to be too mundane to be of interest to me and so remained unspoken. The participants' assurances to me that they wished to contribute to the research, and my interest in the subject, may have led to them seeking to tell me only what they thought would be interesting to me. At times I recognised my disinterest in what the participants were saying to me and I wondered if this was an indication of what the participants were conveying – perhaps their own disinterest in the routine and repetitive daily tasks and demands of childcare. However, this was not spoken and therefore remains a speculative and subjective curiosity on my part.

When I was more curious in descriptions of the antics of the children than of the mother, it was important that I reoriented my interest to the mother because I had informed each mother that my interest was in her experiences and not in those of her children. This means that when considering narratives about the children I considered them in relation to what the mother may be telling me about the implications they have for her. If the mothers spoke about their children and their behaviour with their children in ways that differed to ways I try to be with my children, I sought to recognise the challenge this posed to me and to utilise the mothers' words in the advancement of my knowledge of the experiences of mothers and not to revert to feelings of judgement or criticism.

I hope that my efforts to employ a positive ethical approach in these ways have respected and honoured the desire of the women to speak and be heard in a safe environment created between my role as researcher and mother and their roles as participants and mothers.

The ethical researcher recognises that by seeking meanings in data provided by other people brings with it a responsibility for recognising the inherent power in this process. They recognise that by adding something new to data and generating something new in information that they have seen, heard or read they are shaping what comes to be known about it (Willig, 2012). When the data are numbers and measures provided by participants, the ethical researcher can ensure that participants are aware of the purposes of the test, what is expected of them in carrying out the tests and what will be done with the results of the tests. When the data are words and actions of others, the ethical researcher can choose to involve the participant in the analysis, perhaps by asking for their feedback on interpretations they have made of it or by making explicit the theories they have brought to the data to find meanings within it. In all research the way that the research is presented to wider audiences lies in the hands of the researcher too, so the ethical researcher will be clear about what they have chosen to report and what they have left out, as well as about the framing of the report and the audience it is intended for.

Aims of the book

This book has arisen from experience of conducting, teaching and supervising research using many methods, sometimes singly and sometimes pluralistically, sometimes alone, and often with teams, and in settings that have been academic, clinical and business. Over the years, questions of practice, theory and method have arisen at ever-decreasing intervals. Some of these questions have queried how to best select a method; others have queried how best to employ it; still others have queried how best to support others in their research. Throughout there have been questions about the strengths and limitations of different methods, paradigms and research approaches, but there have also been many questions about the people conducting the research, in which I have included myself. With a wealth of literature to consult, both my own and within institutions, I have looked often for advice and guidance about being a researcher. There is a lot about – usually found in books with the word 'reflective' in the title, and usually focusing on one aspect of the research process. For me, however, this is not enough. Being reflective about one's research practice seems vitally important from its inception to its final presentation. Doing so enhances the quality of the research and its ethical position. However, the word seems so widely used now that it seems to risk becoming a tick-box concern for some researchers and something to avoid for others. For those in the middle of this spectrum there are many questions about what it actually means to be reflective consistently throughout the research process. Undoubtedly it is a key aim of this book to help to unpick this word and its use and implications in all research practice.

The focus on the researcher seems important for many reasons pertinent to research: to understand what research topics are of interest to society, to understand what the impact of research training and skills acquisition means for the development of research questions, to understand why individuals choose to do research, and to understand how those who do research influence the knowledge available to the world. All of these issues can be addressed by thinking about who a researcher is, what they do, and how they do it as part of the assessment of the relevance and credibility of the research itself. A second aim of this book is to lay out the roles of the researcher, and to emphasise their involvement in research from its beginning to its end (or endings). Achieving this aim will mean that researchers are more aware of why they are doing the research they are doing, and those who use research will be able to contextualise it by considering the motivations and agendas that have been brought to it.

The researcher's experience of the research is also relevant to enhancing research quality and usefulness. The influence of affect and emotion on decision-making, and subjectivity is often under-considered in research practice (Zinn, 2006). The research process necessitates a number of planned and unplanned decisions as it develops. These may be decisions about forming the research question, who to recruit as participants, or how to design the study. They may also be prompted by unexpected findings, problems in progressing the research, or personal experiences within or outside the research itself. All of these factors are resolved or not by the researcher, and thus awareness of their experience adds to the critique that can be brought to research and its practice by those conducting it and by those who use it. If sensitive research topics are the focus of inquiry, researchers may find themselves overwhelmed or distressed by the research process. All of this plays into the subjective influence that researchers bring to the process, and a third aim of this book is to highlight these possibilities and enable researchers to equip themselves with tips and strategies that can help to confront and negotiate them.

A fourth aim is to bring all the considerations of the researcher, their role and their impact into a picture that includes all research approaches. For a long time there has been a divide between quantitative and qualitative research, with arguments based largely on scientific status and research outcome credibility. Whilst this divide is seeing some blurring of its boundaries, marked by mixed-methods and pluralistic research approaches, the training and education that many aspiring researchers receive still focuses on a separation of the approaches. There is much literature available about arguments of epistemological incoherence and other paradigmatic assumptions about mixing methods, and is not the focus of this book. Instead the book aims to blur the divide by arguing throughout that a researcher is part of all research, regardless of paradigm or method. Instead of focusing on arguments of different techniques and approaches, the book aims to focus on arguments, conundrums and challenges that, it argues, face all researchers as they strive to conduct good research that will be of use to others.

Structure of the book

The book is organised into six chapters. The first three – this one, Researcher Positionality, and Researcher as Instrument – set the scene for why the researcher is important in all research. The next chapter focuses on being one of a team of researchers and highlights how many of the issues discussed are brought, negotiated and challenged by researching within a team. Chapter 5 considers 'Researching the Self, Researching one's self by discussing the uses of this in research and professional practice. The final chapter closes the book with reflections on how greater understanding of the researcher role, its changes and its impact, enhance and inhibit research practice. It considers how raising awareness and deepening understanding has influenced contemporary research and is leading to new prospects, problems and quality criteria emerging in each of the major research approaches.

Each chapter is organised into key sections and all are complemented with research examples for illustration and discussion. Researcher Views, gathered through interviews with and reflections and ideas from a range of researchers, provide personal insight into conducting research. Reflective Questions encourage further thinking about issues raised in the chapters and are scattered throughout. Each chapter begins with an introduction that will inform readers of what they can expect to learn from reading it and ends with a summary of the key points. At the end of each chapter there is also a list of tips and strategies for improving research practice and a Further Reading list to supplement the full list of References provided at the end of the book. In recognition of the particular language that each research approach has developed, a Glossary is also provided at the end of the book. Words included in the Glossary are indicated in bold throughout the book.

This book can be dipped in and out of as a reference book, or read as an essential textbook for those learning how to conduct research and perhaps embarking on their first research project. However it is used, it will provide a solid foundation for considering the researcher and using awareness of the researcher in research that you conduct or read. This will enhance the quality of your research and the critique you bring to other people's research.

Reflective Question: Why do you do research?

RESEARCHER AS AUTHOR: REFLECTION ON WRITING THE BOOK

I came to consider myself a researcher when working within psychiatric hospitals during training to become a psychodynamic counsellor. Despite an educational background in physics and then psychology I had seen myself learning to become a practitioner concerned with doing things with people rather than as a researcher finding out things with people. When I began to put my learning into practice, however, I very quickly realised that to practice was to find out about people. It wasn't long before my desire to find out about and understand people, for me, extended beyond sitting with them in consulting rooms to wanting to know what knowledge others had gained that could help me in my practice. I had questions about my practice, about my clients and about the models and techniques of counselling that I used that could not be ethically addressed by experimenting with my clients.

I found reading other people's research helpful and interesting but was often left with further questions of my own at the end of it: Why did they focus on this aspect of the topic? What motivated them to do this research? How did they see their research contributing to wider practice?

Eventually deciding to pursue my interest in research, and in people, I studied for a PhD under the supervision of expert, knowledgeable and very supportive supervisors. They recognised that my training in traditional scientific methods of research, combined with my personal interest in people, could make for a rewarding experience of learning and conducting qualitative research. But even this approach was not enough to answer my questions about who the researcher is and how their impact on the research they do can be understood and valued. In learning to be a researcher myself, I sought to use my own self-awareness and desire not to impose my experiences on to those of my research participants, to develop a pluralistic approach to the research I conducted. In the years in which I have subsequently taught this and other forms of research to students, I have discovered that many others have similar questions to me: Why am I doing this research? Does it make a difference that it's me and not someone else doing this research? Would someone else do this research differently? Furthermore, that the answers to all these questions are almost invariably 'Yes'. So then the questions become: What is it about me that means I am doing this research? What do participants see of me in the research? How do I keep myself both within and separate from the research?

And so the idea of the book was born. I wanted a platform that extended beyond lecture theatres and seminar rooms, on which to share the ideas, thoughts, suggestions and inspirations that have come to me and been given to me as I have conducted and taught research. In writing the book many of the same questions have arisen: Why am I writing this book and not someone else? Would someone else write this book differently? What difference do I want this book to make? But as the book developed I also recognised the importance of bringing rigour, soundness and credibility to it, much as is important in research. All through its writing the thought that it will be its usefulness that will define its value has stayed in my mind. I wait to see how it takes its place in the minds and on the shelves of researchers.

Further reading

Bolton, G. (2010). *Reflective practice: Writing and professional development.* Thousand Oaks, CA: Sage Publications. This book provides comprehensive discussion and practical tips for writing reflexively, and the benefits that this can bring to professional practice.

Creswell, J. W. (2013). *Research design: Qualitative quantitative and mixed methods approaches.* Thousand Oaks, CA: Sage Publications. This book describes a number of models of research design in a clear and accessible format.

Etherington, K. (2004). *Becoming a reflexive researcher: Using our selves in research.* London: Jessica Kingsley Publishers. This book draws on conversations and research diaries to show reflexive research in counselling and psychotherapy practice, highlighting how it can enable personal transformation for practitioners and empower clients to take agency over their lives.

Frost, N. A. (Ed.) (2011). *Qualitative research methods in psychology: Combining core approaches.* Maidenhead: Open University Press. This book describes the use of four commonly used qualitative methods (grounded theory, Foucauldian discourse analysis, narrative analysis and interpretative phenomenological analysis), separately and in combination, using examples and personal experience throughout.

Hesse-Biber, S. (Ed.) (2014). *Feminist research practice: A primer.* Thousand Oaks, CA: Sage Publications. This book presents a series of chapters that describe a range of feminist research methods used to explore topics that affect women's lives.

Researcher positionality

2

Chapter map and outcomes

This chapter introduces the notion of **researcher positionality**. It describes some of the ways in which researchers can construct and be constructed into various positions of friendship, expert, collaborator, stakeholder, insider and outsider as the research develops. It draws on theories, methods and empirical examples to illustrate the importance of researchers recognising their positions and how these can change during the research process. The influence of positionality, its flexibility throughout the research process and ways in which its recognition can enhance the quality of research are discussed. By considering a range of research topics, settings and agendas, this chapter allows the reader to understand what positionality is, how it relates to being a researcher and why it is important to understand its role. Following a description of positionality, the chapter uses research examples to consider insider/outsider positions, objective positionality and its challenges, positionality within stakeholder research and policy development, positionality when researching experiences similar to one's own and positionality when researching experiences that researchers have no personal knowledge of. A range of research examples, researcher reflections and problem-based questions are included throughout the chapter and it concludes with a list of tips and strategies that will enable all researchers to consider positionality as part of all research they conduct.

By the end of the chapter, readers will:

- Understand what positionality is and why it is important to researchers
- Be able to identify different positionalities and ways in which they can be provoked in the research process

- Know ways in which positionality can influence researchers
- Have had opportunities to reflect on the role of positionality in research they are conducting
- Be equipped with a range of strategies and tips for recognising their own positionality in their research activities.

Introduction: Defining positionality and its relevance to research

Researcher View

'Um, but it's a very intimate experience and I imagine that the people who were interviewed also remember it because they wouldn't normally do that, and many people say they have never talked about their childhood, so it was kind of privileged information.... I think a good interview is a very intimate experience, sort of sharing minds really.'

Positionality is the personal perspective on events and experiences that is shaped by the unique mix of a person's race, class, gender, ability, sexuality and other dimensions of their identity. The ways in which a person positions themselves, or is positioned by others, informs the ways in which they acquire, interpret and generate knowledge. Knowledge acquired may be chosen because a person considers it appropriate or correct for the position they have constructed. The availability of knowledge is usually constrained by different contexts. Interpretation of knowledge may be informed by personal history, motivation and other aims behind the processes of knowledge gathering and access. Both knowledge acquisition and interpretation are key to how a person understands the world and chooses to present themselves as part of it to others. Think, for example, of how a new mother may describe difficulties she is experiencing in motherhood to another mother, to her partner, to a close friend and to her own mother. All accounts may be shaped by how the mother perceives and positions each of these people and the expectations she has about how they are going to receive and make sense of what she is telling them. She will also be aware of cultural and historical understandings of what mothers are supposed to be like, and these will shape how she presents and positions herself to others.

Reflective Question: What positions do you occupy in a typical day in your life? Think about your roles as a student, a friend, a partner, an employee, a carer and so on. How does your positionality change with tasks you perform as the day progresses?

A person's affect and emotion when they are seeking, acquiring and interpreting knowledge also contribute to their positionality. Diversity in moral and political perspectives can lead to people feeling different from others and experiencing discomfort in acquiring knowledge that may not accord with their own view of the world, how it is or how they think it should be. Dealing with emotions can present challenges to a person's positionality, depending not only on what those emotions are but also on the context and setting in which they are provoked and experienced. Think, for example, of how someone who is homosexual may feel when discussing it with a friend and when visiting a country where homosexuality is forbidden.

Researcher positionality is the myriad positions that researchers can adopt or be perceived by participants as adopting, during the research process. Having an awareness of positionality, and how it can change, helps researchers to provide insight into why and how data has been elicited and gathered from participants and how this has influenced its interpretation. Researcher positionality is important in all aspects of the research process because it informs both the questions asked and the ways that the study is carried out.

Positionality awareness

In feminist research, researcher positionality is considered in light of dimensions such as gender, age, class, sexuality, dis/ability and other personal dimensions that are shaped by the context in which they are lived. Feminist researchers recognise the inherent role that their own personal dimensions play in conducting and constructing research and consider how these inform and shape the research process.

Feminist researchers seek to flatten hierarchies within research and its processes. Hierarchies may be between the researcher and the researched, between the research conduct and its dissemination or between the research aims and the status given to it by a wider audience. A 'hierarchy of evidence' within biomedical research prioritises experimental and pseudo-experimental research designs and ranks anecdotal evidence and expert opinion as at the bottom. Feminist researchers argue that all such hierarchies give too much status to objective generalisable research methods, do not allow for certain research questions to be asked and constrain how information and understanding of other people is obtained. In practice, much, although importantly not all, feminist research is qualitative in its approach (see discussion of feminist objectivity and strong objectivity later in this chapter). It aims to seek out descriptions of experience directly from those that have had the experience and to interpret meanings within the descriptions that recognise the limitations of the knowledge available to the researcher as well as to the researched, and how these are informed by the relationship between them.

Approaches such as the memory-work method offer one way to address the hierarchy between the researcher and the researched. Memory work (Haug, 1987) recognises the power dynamics in research relationships and seeks to flatten them completely by advocating that the researcher becomes the researched. Collectives of researchers are formed to explore and examine meanings of personal memories of the group members, evoked in response to an agreed trigger. The researchers aim to understand how the memory contributes to the construction of the memory owner by exploring it from personal and group subjective stances and from social structure perspectives. This approach aims to understand not only how individuals (women, in the original studies) construct themselves but also how they reinforce constructions imposed by wider contexts of politics, history and society.

In other research practices the researcher seeks to maintain an openness to the questioning of them by research participants, to make clear to the participants their interest and aims in researching the topic and also to invite the questioning of their approach and taken-for-granted assumptions about knowledge. Researchers adopt a reflexive stance, to bring transparency to their motivation for the research and their role throughout it and to consider the impact of the researcher on the research process. Such ethical care reduces the imposition of researcher bias on to the research process and enhances the credibility of the research outcomes.

Many feminist researchers have claimed that their personal experiences have driven the nature of the research topic (David, Weiner, & Arnot, 1996). This can be beneficial to the research in ensuring that the complexity of participants' experiences is better heard and interpreted but there is also the risk of competing discourses challenging researcher positionality. The long history of feminist research being embedded in the idea of personal autobiography, and that 'the personal is political', also raises the question of legitimacy for feminist researchers who have not had personal experiences of the topic they are investigating (Frost & Holt, 2014, see later in this chapter for more on this).

Feminist approaches to research are not confined to qualitative and explicitly subjective research. 'Strong objectivity' (Harding, 1991) describes research orientated to feminist perspectives. It aims to begin research from the perspective of lives of women and questions what knowledge is objective, whether objectivity is necessary and if it is possible to achieve objectivity. For Harding these concerns were based on sexism and androcentric bias in dominant scientific studies.

Strong objectivity has been brought to research practice in a range of arenas that include business and management practice, healthcare provision and education. Across all domains, and regardless of the subjective/objective stance of the research methodology, strong objectivity requires the researcher to consider what lies behind the research hypotheses and questions, and the way that the research has been shaped to inquire into it. This places the researcher within the research, both as co-constructor of the research with the participants and in the development of its design and the interpretation and reporting of its data.

> **Reflective Question**: Does it matter whether researchers adopting a feminist stance are women or not? Think about what topics can be researched using feminist approaches and reasons why these topics can benefit from a feminist research approach.

Positionality and the objective researcher

In traditional scientific research, approaches based on hypothesis and theory testing, the researcher aims to be neutral in their interaction with participants and objective in the ways that the data is analysed and interpreted. Researchers seek to position themselves as an observer who is outside the research process, in the belief that this minimises subjective bias they may bring to it. However, if we consider that researcher affect and emotion can be influenced by the topic under study, the context in which the study is being conducted and the motivation for carrying out the study, it is easy to see that at the very least the researcher may be challenged to maintain a position as someone unaffected by distressing data, unexpected results or participants who do not fit the category within which they have been recruited.

As one experienced researcher of sexual abuse of children put it:

They made a huge impact on me when I first started [clinical] interviewing. I would carry these interviews around with me for years in my head.

Objective researchers do recognise researcher positionality but couch it in different terms: **experimenter bias**, in which a researcher's cognitive bias causes them to unconsciously influence the responses of the participant, and **participant demand characteristics**, in which participants form an interpretation of the experimenter's purpose and unconsciously change their behaviour to fit that interpretation. For objective researchers these are key criteria to be aware of in assessing the reliability and validity of the results obtained. They are accounted for and controlled in experimental studies but findings that researchers demonstrate unconscious behaviours in their body language and linguistic communication that can influence the study at all stages challenge the extent to which they can be managed.

Often conducted under laboratory conditions with carefully controlled variables, experimental research may not at first appear to need to pay attention to positionality of the researcher; however, a small body of work has emerged to challenge this assumption.

Within experimental research the notion of 'experimenter bias' has been recognised and discussed (e.g. Rosenthal, 1963, 1967), usually in precautionary terms. Experimenter bias can be defined as conscious or unconscious biasing of the data and its analysis towards desired results. The bias arises from cues emanating from the experimenter through non-verbal communication, or in paralinguistic cues such as tone of voice that differ across the data collection and groups. Originating within animal learning studies, researchers found that apparent phenomena such as that of Clever Hans (e.g. Sebeok & Rosenthal, 1981), a horse that appeared to be able to solve mathematical problems and 'read' and answer a variety of verbal questions put to it by researchers, could be explained by the animal's ability to detect aspects of human behaviour that gave away the answers (Chevalier-Skolnikoff, 1981). These included slight inclinations of the questioners' heads and bodies. In the sociology discipline, Merton (1948) introduced the concept of the 'self-fulfilling prophecy' in which the influence of one person's behaviour over another's is altered because of the perceived expectations of the behaviour.

Such findings raise the issue for the objective researcher as to whether mistaken inferences in the results have arisen because of unintended treatment of participants and whether the tensions between the expectations and the independent variable of interest have been confounded to the extent that they make the results uninterpretable. Awareness of issues such as these have led to important work in health and education practitioners' behaviour so that, for example, expectations by teachers of particular students can influence academic performance, for better or for worse (see Rosenthal & Jacobson, 1968). It is not hard to imagine how the influence of researcher expectations can play a role in how psychotherapists or healthcare providers working face-to-face with clients may respond to questions about their practice or success rates.

In efforts to adhere to the scientific canon of objectivity, awareness of such cues without attending to them is regarded as potentially unscrupulous researcher behaviour and unethical research practice. Of course if the cues are deliberately introduced to support operationalisation of independent variables by deviating from prescribed practice, the research practice is unethical and researchers can be trained to recognise and eliminate such behaviours. It is potentially more challenging, however, for the researcher seeking objectivity to acknowledge that unconscious cues may emanate from them and affect the research.

To some extent these can be addressed with heightened awareness of the need for agreed procedures, forms of questioning and statistical interpretation of data to be adhered to. However, it may also be useful for the objective researcher to also consider their subjective aims and motivations in conducting the research. This can begin at the outset of the research process by considering what literature they have chosen to formulate the study, who they have chosen to recruit for it and how the potential participants have been approached. During the data-collection phases, however, awareness by the researcher of their engagement with the topic, of how their personal experiences may be similar or very different from the participants', of feelings associated with these, and of strategies they may employ if they find their minds or bodies turning to these experiences and feelings during the course of the data collection, can enhance the research practice.

The following summary of a study of potentially depressed and non-depressed Irish-born migrants living in London conducted by Ryan and Golden (2006) illustrates how researchers can be positioned by participants in ways they had not anticipated.

RESEARCH EXAMPLE

Summary of research from L. Ryan & A. Golden (2006). Tick the box please: A reflexive approach to doing quantitative social research. *Sociology, 40*(6), 1191–1200.

(Continued)

Study aim: To investigate the differences between Irish-born migrants living in London who had been identified as potentially depressed and those not potentially depressed.

The researchers: Two Irish-born female researchers who had moved to Britain in the 1990s to pursue academic careers. One (Ryan) is a sociologist with a particular interest in feminist theory who had conducted a qualitative study of Irish migrant women using a life-narrative approach. The other (Golden) is a health psychologist who had previously worked on a health-related quantitative study within a department of epidemiology using advanced statistical modelling to analyse large data sets.

The participants: 442 male and female participants ranging in age from 18 to 80 years were initially identified and contacted through their local GP practice. They were divided into a control group (those identified as not potentially depressed) and a case group (those identified as potentially depressed). Dates, times and venues for meeting with the researchers were arranged by telephone.

Methods: A short postal questionnaire was first distributed to each participant, which was followed up by a longer 14-page questionnaire administered in person by the researchers. This addressed demographic information, health status, a psychiatric screening instrument, current social support, experiences of childhood trauma and migration to Britain. Participants were offered a choice of venues but most chose to be interviewed in their own homes. Interviews lasted between 45 minutes and one hour.

Findings: There were various findings in relation to the differences between those participants who were potentially depressed and those who were not (see Ryan, Leavey, Golden, Blizzard & King, 2006) but Ryan and Golden were also interested to find that the personal administration of the questionnaire meant that many of the respondents also told them stories about their migration to Britain. The stories provided more nuanced and detailed information than the tick-box approach of the questionnaire allowed for.

As the stories were told the researchers realised that they were being identified by the questionnaire respondents as Irish migrants. Although they had not disclosed this the respondents had recognised their Irish heritage from their accents. The stories developed when the questions of belonging to host countries and return to home countries were asked. The stories usually focused on the dilemmas the respondents faced about remaining in Britain and returning to Ireland. The researchers report that these dilemmas were real issues for them, too, and they found themselves invited by the participants to share their own sense of belonging, as Irish migrants talking to other Irish migrants rather than as researchers collecting data from respondents. This presented some difficulties and upset to the researchers because they felt the dilemmas keenly and personally. They report also feeling, at times, led by respondents into providing them with company and friendship.

Conclusions: The researchers' experiences of the study meant that they found they could not detach themselves from the topic. Many of the questions they asked touched on personal experiences and their sense of self as migrants. At these times it was hard to maintain a neutral researcher stance and instead they were positioned as Irish migrants. Awareness of this positionality and the impact it had on the data collection led them to develop a second qualitative study using the additional data. They stress the need to recognise and reflect on the emotional cost of research from the design stage and the potential to add depth of understanding about how, where, when and by whom data are collected.

The study illustrates the difficulty in maintaining detachment and objectivity in research that touches on personal experiences and identities of researchers. These researchers found that the usual physical, temporal, ethical and socio-cultural boundaries between researcher and researched that need to be overcome in order to objectively communicate participant knowledge, opinions, feelings and experiences shifted in the course of this research, influencing the type of data collected and the researchers' experiences of the research study.

Their positionality can be seen to fluctuate from researcher to migrant to friend in a dynamic process that the researchers had some but not total influence over. By recognising the social boundaries and how they can shift during research that calls for detachment, these researchers argue that depth of insight can be enhanced and strategies for anticipating, negotiating and sharing such experiences included in the research design without detriment to the research process or outcomes.

For the objective researcher conducting research into sensitive topics, a similar awareness may be applied to understand how preparation and debriefing of participants are offered at the beginning and conclusion of the study. Salient topics may provoke emotionality within researchers who are interested only in measuring or testing theories and hypotheses. The issue then becomes about what such 'objective' researchers choose to do with this awareness in regard to the conduct of their research.

The objective researcher who finds themselves experiencing emotions they had not anticipated on meeting participants can ask themselves questions about age, gender, class, sexual orientation and physical abilities and the knowledge and assumptions about such dimensions they may hold. Simple reflexive issues such as these may better prepare the objective researcher for delivering more standardised procedures and for holding an awareness of the possibility and actualities of experiencing affect and emotion during the research process that they then may be better able to deal with outside of the research process, thus minimising their impact on it.

Positionality and the subjective researcher

Researcher View

'I think I tend to learn things best by actually experiencing them and I think most people are similar, but you know that to actually go through something and be in that situation I think is a much better way of learning about something than kind of trying to read about it.'

Subjective researchers make researcher positionality as explicit as possible to meet a key quality criterion of the qualitative research process. This is because the social identities and positionalities of the researcher in the research process are seen to confer a status on the researcher that influences the ways in which the communication during the data-gathering phases and the subsequent interpretation of the data occur. The power of the individuals involved in the process is seen to be enabled or limited by the positionality conferred on them or adopted by them. Awareness of the researcher positionality and the ways in which it changes during the research promotes an understanding of and response to the changing balance of power that pervades and impacts on the research process (Lavis, 2010). Such an awareness not only makes more explicit the ways in which power relations enacted during the study have informed the ways that knowledge has been gained and disseminated but also enhances the trustworthiness and transparency of the ways in which it has been reached.

Several subjective researchers have highlighted the role and influence of emotionality in their work. In qualitative research this is regarded as an opportunity to consider its influence on the research process. Researchers recognise that emotionality can lead to absences in their behaviours with participants. They may close down further questioning about a subject they are experiencing difficulties with or unconsciously withhold non-verbal communication such as eye contact with the participant. A sense of awkwardness may develop in the interaction with the participant and consequent embarrassment on both sides can influence the rapport between them.

> **Reflective Question:** How will you know whether you have been affected by research you are conducting? Think about what happens not only during the research but also after it. Apart from conscious feelings and emotions, what else might indicate an effect of the research on you?

Positionality and the mixed-methods researcher

For those researchers who use both quantitative and qualitative approaches and methods in their work, mixed-methods researchers, there can be a tension in how and when to consider their own positionality. This can arise from the challenges of adopting a neutral objective researcher stance alongside a reflexive subjective stance. The example from Ryan and Golden (2006) above shows the impact of this and not only that efforts to position oneself as a researcher can be challenged by participants but also that seeking to remain outside the research can be hampered by personal characteristics and perception by others, which are not always anticipated by researchers.

The mixed-methods researcher will use one or more methods drawn from qualitative and quantitative approaches to investigate their topic of inquiry in pursuit of insights and findings that could not otherwise be reached. This means that they have to position themselves both as a neutral observer of the research and as an active co-constructor of it, in order to incorporate the methodological assumptions of both qualitative and quantitative approaches.

By seeking to use mixed methods in their research, researchers are combining world views that on the one hand consider their research to lead to one universal truth and on the other provide access to the unique perspectives brought to the understanding of experience by individuals and groups. Holding such contrasting views simultaneously can lead to challenges arising from not only the training and education about methods and research approaches that individual researchers have had but also how they will position themselves to acquire the knowledge they seek. This means that their views of the ways in which knowledge is constructed and by whom are challenged as they interchange between methods and approaches. As an example, consider research into the gender–wage gap.

RESEARCH EXAMPLE

Summary of research from L. M. Roth (2006). *Selling women short: Gender and money on Wall Street*. Princeton, NJ: Princeton University Press.

This study aimed to identify structural factors within the workplace that may contribute to gender–wage gaps on Wall Street. Seventy-six equally qualified men and women who worked on Wall Street were interviewed about their career history from before their qualification up to the time of the interview, their daily experiences in the workplace, the number of hours worked, salaries earned over time, job conditions and performance evaluations. The interviews were semi-structured and included both closed and open-ended questions.

The quantitative data identified and revealed the extent of the wage gap. The qualitative data enabled understanding of the processes that might have contributed to this. Underlying organisation structures that were accessed through this approach revealed unarticulated and unconscious practices such as employers seeking out traits in employees that are believed to be more masculine than feminine and bonus systems that did not allow for maternity-leave breaks in career development. Prioritising the qualitative component of the research enabled access to subjugated knowledge provided in accounts of everyday experience that gave insight into the inner workings of the workplace environment. The research design necessitated the researcher to consider the value of the quantitative component of the study and how it enhanced the qualitative findings.

Roth (2006) used a combination of closed and open questions in a mixed-methods design that sought factual information about wages over time, bonuses and performance evaluations, and accounts of everyday experiences of women working on Wall Street in the 1980s. The combination of data that she gained allowed her to collate factual information about how women employees were rewarded and acknowledged and insight into what it was like to strive to achieve these rewards in this male-dominated environment. This researcher clearly delineated the types of information she was seeking in her research and structured her questions accordingly. She found that there were detrimental differences to the women in both the rewards and recognition they gained, and their experiences of this, but that some of these differences arose from institutional practices and structures that served to inhibit women's progression compared to that of men.

Were the study to have been only a qualitative approach, the focus on reflexivity and the ways in which the researcher may construct research questions, elicit and analyse data and how she chose to write it up would have been made explicit. Were the study to have been purely quantitative in gathering facts about wages and performance evaluation, she may have chosen to administer the closed questions electronically or by post to maintain a neutral stance. In using the two approaches together this researcher must have considered questions such as her own experiences of wage difference and why she is interested in researching the topic in an environment different to her own academic one. Ryan and Golden suggest that mixed-methods researchers may have to be selective about when they apply criteria such as reflexivity, often at the start and conclusion of the study (2006). In this way the assessment of the quality of the research demonstrates the awareness of positionality that the researcher brings to it and applies it to those parts of the study where it is most accessible.

Although mixed-methods research can take many forms, one that is becoming increasingly common has been labelled **pragmatic research** (e.g. Onwuegbuzie & Leech, 2005). This movement arose in recognition of the divisive and damaging effect on research that adherence to the use of either quantitative or qualitative methods can result in. It highlights that the researchers on either side of this apparent divide see themselves in competition with each other, positioning themselves as researchers who are either purists or situationalists (Onwuegbuzie & Leech, 2005). This in turn can lead to feelings of alienation by researchers of the different group and is reinforced by the terminology used by writers from both disciplines. For example much of the language associated with quantitative research relies on conventions of notation and terminology not used in everyday life (Onwuegbuzie, DaRos, & Ryan, 1997). Similarly, the language of qualitative research has introduced terms such as reflexivity and trustworthiness as quality criteria. These represent not only the reinforcement of differences between the two approaches but also practical challenges for the researcher in evaluating research that mixes methods.

Repositioning themselves as pragmatic enables researchers to be collaborative and flexible in their acceptance of philosophical orientations. Some writers have argued that pragmatic researchers are more likely to view the research as a holistic endeavour that requires them to engage with it over time and with persistent observation (e.g. Lincoln & Guba, 1985; Newman & Benz, 1998). Onwuegbuzie (2003) argues that pragmatic researchers are more able to position themselves as researchers who can combine empirical precision with descriptive precision, being more able to zoom into microscopic detail as well as zoom out to macro levels of detail by viewing the research with a bifocal lens instead of a single lens.

The key consideration for the positionality of the mixed-methods researcher therefore seems to be that it is the methodological assumptions that they bring to the research that must also drive their subjective positioning as researchers. This has to be considered as well as the ways in which their identities other than researcher are made salient throughout the research process.

Preparing for the dynamism of researcher positionality can add to the toolbox of researcher preparation and research conduct and enhances the quality of the research being conducted. Researchers can be positioned by participants, contexts and topics in ways they had not expected or anticipated. How the research process is conducted, and the data collected as a consequence of this, can be useful and beneficial to the research. In the next section, the chapter will consider how recognition of positionality can be used at the outset of the research to design the study and recruit participants. It will discuss how these plans can be challenged and modified as the identified positions are renegotiated by participants and context, regardless of the methodology employed in the research study.

Insider/outsider researchers

Many researchers choose to position themselves as either an 'outsider' or an 'insider' of the community in which they are conducting the research. The construction of a researcher as an insider or an outsider is made by their notions of self and the participants' views of them. Insider constructions may be influenced by perceived similarity in dimensions such as race, class, gender, sexuality and so on, or by shared experiences and perceptions of the world. Outsider researcher constructions arise from perceived lack of overlaps in personal or experiential categories. The research example above illustrated how the participants' recognition of and reaction to the researchers as Irish migrants led to them being positioned as insiders (Irish migrants) when they had set out to position themselves as outsiders (researchers). Insider/outsider positioning by participants is developed from a range of dimensions that can include gender, shared knowledge assumptions (assuming that the researcher has experienced what is being described to them) and shared understandings of historical and social influences (such as the role of women in Western society).

In addition to being positioned by participants, researchers can choose how to position themselves to the benefit of the research. The outsider researcher position is always present in the research and needs to be there in order to ensure rigorous and systematic research but researchers may additionally position themselves as insiders of particular groups so that they can utilise networks to approach and engage potential participants and gain nuanced knowledge. Insider/

outsider positioning influences from the outset how researchers are perceived in the research process and, as the following research example shows, can challenge researchers' own perceptions of their positions within groups.

RESEARCH EXAMPLE

Summary of research from D. Ganga & S. Scott (2006). Cultural 'insiders' and the issue of positionality in qualitative migration research: Moving 'across' and moving 'along' researcher-participant divides. *Forum: Qualitative Social Research*, 7(3).

Aims: To understand insider positionality when research is conducted using social interviews conducted between researchers and participants who share a similar cultural, linguistic, ethnic, national and religious heritage.

Two studies were conducted: one with a group of skilled British migrants living in Paris (Scott), the other with individuals drawn from two generations of Italian families living in Nottingham (Ganga).

The researchers: Both researchers had the same ethnonational backgrounds as the participants in their studies.

Methods: Scott conducted a study of a skilled first-generation British migrant community in Paris by mapping their residential distribution across Paris, examining motives underpinning British emigration to Paris, exploring and explaining the British communality observed and identifying the different migration types resident in Paris. Thirty-six in-depth interviews, a survey of 110 British organisations based in Paris and visits to a selected number of these organisations to observe and participate in their activities were carried out.

Ganga conducted a study to explore ethnic self-perception of the children and grandchildren of ten Italian families who arrived in the Nottingham area in the 1950s and 1960s. Semi-structured interviews were conducted using a list of topics identified in advance, with questions differentiated according to the generation of the participants. Question types included biographical, behavioural/experiential and attitudinal/belief.

Findings: Class and the Migrant Interview: By positioning themselves as cultural insiders, the researchers had advantages such as negotiating access to migrants, understanding the spoken and unspoken language of the research interview and recognising idiosyncratic cultural references. Internal divisions within the migrant community (referred to as the 'imagined migrant community' by the researchers) were better enabled to be brought to the fore to allow the researcher to gain greater understanding of the reasons for the differences.

(Continued)

Disadvantages included an enhanced awareness of differences in researcher and participant social positions constructed by intersections of class, generation, age and gender. For Scott, a student, the socio-economic class divide between him and the participants was keenly felt by recognising the 'elite' residential areas the participants lived in, the high salaries they earned and the relatively exclusive networks in which they moved, all of which were not accessible to him outside his research practice.

Ganga found that her efforts to use her insider status to meet with an Italian Association for Older People of Nottingham, in order to gain access to younger members of families through the first-generation members, were thwarted. The first-generation participants had perceptions of what it meant to be Italian that were different to those of the researcher and sought to act as gatekeepers of access to the second- and third-generation potential respondents, thus removing the selection of participants from the researcher's control. Privacy and the threats to the privacy of members of their families were also prominent amongst the first-generation participants and highlighted that the researcher was regarded by them as a researcher rather than as an insider to their group.

Conclusions: Ganga and Scott (2006) use the term 'diversity in proximity' (2006, p. 2) to describe how their assumed positions as insiders enabled them to better recognise 'both the ties that bind us and the social fissures that divide us' (p. 2). Setting out with the belief that they could legitimately position themselves as insiders of each group, Scott found issues related to the influence of class that he had not foreseen, and for Ganga of her age being an issue in recruiting and gathering data from participants within the same families. Although regarding himself as an insider to the group that he was studying Scott had not anticipated the influence of class and wealth on the power dynamics of the interviews. He had not known that this group existed and had never met people from such privileged backgrounds. As a postgraduate student conducting research he found himself asking how it would be possible to 'move up' the socio-economic scale and bridge the divide. He concluded that he would soon be found out by his participants if he pretended to know and understand their world and instead sought to use shared commonalities, for example knowledge of shared geographies such as areas of the UK they both knew and shared topics of current political interest to the British community, and to capitalise on the fact that many of his participants had children the same age as him.

Ganga had also positioned herself as an insider by sharing a common Italian heritage with those she interviewed. She found, however, that there was a reticence amongst the older migrants to act as a gateway to access younger members of their family, citing mistrust of strangers and of people from official organisations who may intrude on the privacy of the family. Also, her assumption of shared 'Italianness' (p. 6) was not seen as the same as that of older migrants who had lived in the UK longer than she had, had different values to her about what it meant to be Italian and who did not regard their children/grandchildren as suitable for the research because of their more limited linguistic and cultural knowledge. To address these challenges Ganga describes adopting 'moving across' age and generations to access second- and third-generation offspring of Italian-born migrants who were much closer to her not only in age and generation but also in terms of cultural likenesses and differences in regard to being Italian.

This research example shows that although a researcher can choose to position themselves as an insider at the start of the study and assume that they will understand nuances of language, humour and other cultural references, challenges to their assumptions can arise from discovering unforeseen divisions and fissures within the communities they have positioned themselves in. The positionality of the researcher fluctuates during the research process and influences the power dynamics between the researcher and the participants in the study. A constant renegotiation of insider/outsider positions takes place as the research unfolds.

This fluidity can bring both benefits and threats to the research. Ways of addressing differences in positioning can be found by seeking out topics that cross the divides between researcher and participant and between class, generation and age, by sharing knowledge of relevant events and acknowledging mutual acquaintances (Ganga & Scott, 2006). The constructions of positions by researchers and participants are made from the interpretation and intersections of these dimensions, generated through communication in research interviews, to form perceptions and understandings of associated identities.

Positionality is also constructed from beliefs and values of researchers, and as with the dimensions that are perceived to be fixed such as gender and age, these can intersect and contribute to the fluidity of positionality in the research process. Rather than positioning oneself as a member of the group based on history and heritage, many researchers are interested in researching experiences that they have had themselves or are interested in for other personal reasons. This can bring tensions of encountering differences in interpretation of and actions concerning the experiences because they may cross personal beliefs and values boundaries for the researcher.

It is to this notion that the next section of the chapter now turns. It will first of all consider some of the issues of positionality arising when carrying out research into experiences that a researcher has had themselves. The section will then consider the challenges to researcher positionality when researching unknown experiences. The section will conclude by drawing these together to consider the challenges of managing and negotiating positionality arising from the intersection of personal, professional and methodological dimensions of the researcher self.

Researching experiences the researcher has had themselves

It is not uncommon for researchers to want to find out more about experiences they have had themselves. Chapter 5 will focus on research of one's self as an entity but in this section issues affecting positionality arising from exploring the experiences of others that resonate with personal experiences will be discussed.

Researcher View

'With the importance of conducting good research in order to achieve the funder's requirements, and the need to put aside my practice as a nurse whilst conducting the research I was clear that my role was to position myself as an aspiring academic and not as a healthcare provider.'

The quote above describes how researchers can set out to put aside the personal aspects of themselves that have led them to be interested in a topic and instead to position and present themselves simply as professionals with an academic interest in the experiences of others. As this chapter has shown this is usually impossible to maintain throughout interviews and face-to-face interactions with participants and for this researcher her experiences were no exception:

'I was surprised to find that I was accepted straightaway as a researcher by each participant. None questioned my experience or background. To my further surprise I found myself disclosing to them at various stages of the interview that I had had other careers alongside being a researcher, and also that I was about to get married.'

Although this researcher was surprised, the readers of this chapter may not be surprised to hear that at times the researcher was positioned as a nurse, as a career woman and as a mother. The importance of context in affecting, influencing and changing positionalities can arise from a number of sources. These may be topics under discussion (perhaps care of new babies was being discussed in the interview and resonated with the researcher's experiences as a mother and a nurse) or assumed shared knowledge (perhaps implied in the language used by the participant) to bids for collusion from participants (perhaps by a participant showing distress or a need for advice prompting the researcher to resist positioning herself as a nurse).

What is key to the research is to anticipate and prepare for the shifting positionalities in order to limit adverse effects on the rigour of the research process. In addition to ways already discussed in the chapter that have included utilising the additional data gathered from new positionalities and adopting a reflexive stance to the research, researchers can draw on peer support and methodological tenets to both prepare for and advance the research in the face of shifting positionalities. All of these become particularly important when researching experience one has had oneself so that every step is taken to avoid inadvertently imposing one's own story on to that recounted by others.

The following research example illustrates some of the positions that researchers can inhabit and how they can shift across the research process. In relation to their maternal status, it describes how personal and professional experience can intersect with the desired position of 'researcher' and how recognition of these shifts can improve and aid the research process.

RESEARCH EXAMPLE

Summary of research from N. A. Frost & A. Holt (2014). Mother, researcher, feminist, woman: Reflections on 'maternal status' as a researcher identity. *Qualitative Research Journal*, 14(2), 90–102.

Two studies conducted separately by two researchers evaluated how their maternal status had shaped their role as researchers in research conducted with mothers. One study (Holt's) aimed to explore the experiences of mothers whose children were involved in the youth justice system. The other study (Frost's) explored the transition to second-time motherhood by mothers having a second child. Holt recruited 15 women through parenting co-ordinators based at four Youth Offending Teams, and interviewed each woman once. Frost recruited through parenting networks and interviewed four times at three-monthly intervals seven women who were six months pregnant at the start of the study.

From the outset of the study, maternal status informed the conduct of the study. Holt, a non-mother, relied on statutory services to recruit

(Continued)

participants, Frost, a mother, accessed personal networks to enable snowball recruitment through word of mouth. Holt reported challenges in the data gathering, in which she felt exposed by her lack of mothering experience:

> 'Not only do I know very little about school reports, exclusions, teenage boys, the school run and all those everyday details of parenting, but my lack of understanding the visceral and emotional aspects of the mother–son relationship makes me feel failed as both researcher and woman.'

Frost reported feeling challenged by a perception that she was an 'expert mother' by the participants in her study:

> 'I found this challenging as I certainly did not feel like an expert mother, or even a very experienced one at that stage.'

The researchers employed narrative analysis to explore the construction of identity amongst their participants but acknowledged that this choice also helped them to construct their own positions. As a mother, Frost used it because it best enabled her to remain open to and grounded in the data, to gain insight into how others constructed their identities as mothers preparing to and then having a second child.

> '...developing an open rapport with participants that allowed me to acknowledge shared knowledge about, for example, the difficulties of being constantly awakened by a crying baby during the night. I was also able to be honest with participants on many occasions about what their accounts had triggered in me as a mother.'

As a non-mother, Holt used narrative analysis to enable participants to speak of issues that she knew little about but wondered if it also positioned her more safely as a researcher:

> 'My use of narrative analysis had as much to do with my own lack of professional confidence in knowing "what to ask" parents than any theoretical motivation. Furthermore, is the narrative interview's production of such a taciturn researcher stance "born of defence" by creating a safe place for the researcher which avoids role uncertainty and self-disclosure, as Gough (2003) suggests?'

She reports needing to negotiate the barrier created by not having the experiences being described to her but wanting to demonstrate to participants that she could understand them on some level:

> 'As such, I felt there was a barrier which hindered the way in which I could relate to the participants and I needed to find a way of mediating this and breaking down this barrier, maybe to show that although

I had no "direct experience" that at least I understood on some level where they were coming from.'

Both researchers reported shifting positionalities that intersected with their researcher position. Frost commented on her experience as a counsellor being evoked at times during the study:

'In contrast, I found myself more reluctant to disclose the counsellor in me when I felt positioned that way and on listening back to the tapes often heard myself closing down descriptions by participants of feeling overwhelmed by their emotions when they began to cry or otherwise show distress. Instead I fell back on ethical procedures that prompted me to offer them a break or to terminate the interview.'

Holt positioned herself as a sibling of brothers who had been in trouble with police:

'At times, I attempted to cobble a narrative together by describing how, as a teenager, my brother had been in trouble with the police, and my parents were therefore open to accusations of blame. But this was not why I had chosen the research topic. In fact, my original doctoral proposal aimed to explore the experiences of siblings of young offenders, but two months into my doctoral studies I realised that, with so little theoretical and empirical research on this topic, a switch to examine parenthood would be a more academically fruitful avenue. Thus, ultimately (although perhaps not initially) my research topic choice was strategic rather than personal.'

The quotations have been reproduced with kind permission from Emerald Group Publishing Limited.

The strategies described by these researchers sought to maintain the rigour of the research process in different ways. At its outset the positioning of themselves as 'a researcher' provided a focus on developing a sound theoretical foundation for the study that informed the most appropriate choice of methodology and methods to address the research focus. The inclusion of subjective reflections to guide the process and the decisions taken throughout it, reduced the imposition of personal experience on to the interpretation of the experiences of others, whilst recognising that researchers' personal experiences were evoked by what they were being told. At moments during the data collection when researchers were aware of discomfort in how they were positioned they were better able to make the thinking and interest behind the study more transparent to the participants without at the same time appearing not to know what they were doing in either sphere. When analysing and interpreting the data these researchers were able to recognise intersections with personal experiences and return to the data to seek evidence for their interpretations. Recognising some of the positions they had adopted in the research process, they were able to put aside their own values to conduct more theoretically informed research.

The study shows that the focus of the research can evoke different positions for the researcher who sets out to bring a defined research approach with an awareness of identities they have that are not about being a researcher. At times the positions can feel uncomfortable and lead a researcher to lose confidence in their research practice and in their identity as a researcher. At other times the positions can be informative and help them to draw on knowledge and experience they have in realms other than research. At the heart of the awareness of positionalities lies a recognition that the researcher position is not fixed, yet that it is always necessary to draw on positions to advance the research. These researchers used principles of research practice and personal experiences to elicit knowledge they could bring to the research to promote rapport and to keep the focus of the research on the participants and the data they provide.

Researchers who are asked to carry out research into particular topics for particular reasons face additional questions about their positionality in the process. They may have a stake in the research such as being practitioners who are seeking evidence to enhance practice or researchers seeking information for policy development or implementation. In these cases it is important that wider considerations are given to the research so that all those who may be involved or affected by its outcomes are included and considered in the positions taken up by the researcher. Researchers may additionally be working within limited time frames. The notion of positioning themselves as an insider or an outsider may be less salient or clear and instead the researchers have to find ways to make judgements about the research directions and outcomes that can be crucial to those for whom it is being conducted. The next section considers ways in which the positionality of researchers conducting such research can be managed.

Researcher as stakeholder

Stakeholder researchers are those who have an investment in the research. The investment may be to bring about change or to enable others to implement change. Stakeholder researchers therefore nearly always have their positionality tied to issues of power and resistance and so should strive to raise awareness of tensions and dynamics existing amongst the stakeholders under study.

This may be particularly so for those stakeholder researchers working within small-scale projects or particular policy environments. National policy researchers on the other hand may not be so invested in the policy environments if they are not involved in the specific policy process under investigation or are operating from an independent research base. It is important to remember, however, that these researchers, too, may position themselves and be positioned by other stakeholders as insiders, even if they feel removed from the context of the study.

Whether working individually or as part of a team, the researchers can be either insiders or outsiders. Insiders may be directly involved in the project, its management or the policy under study. Similarly, insiders may be members of the culture or organisation under scrutiny but outsiders to the focus of the research. Of course the position of the researcher informs their potential vested interest in the outcome of the study and so raises again the importance of this being as explicit as possible throughout the research study. The potential for insiders having increased access to participants seems a good reason for utilising these researchers but it is also the case that pre-existing relationships can adversely influence the likelihood of participants agreeing to take part. Consider, for example, a study of policies affecting people with HIV/AIDS or seeking access to other generations of migrant families (Ganga & Scott, 2006 discussed above). Varvasovszky (Varvasovszky & Mckee 1998) highlights that her position as a stakeholder with knowledge of health policies but lack of experience in the field of alcohol policy development meant that she was considered as being able to bring a more objective view to the study. It is suggested then (Brugha & Varvasovszky, 2000) that a mixed team of insider/outsider researchers provides the best opportunity to draw on contextual insights of insiders and to gain insight into how insiders' assumptions may be biasing the analysis of the information gained.

As with all forms of research, stakeholder researcher positions flex as more and less salient topics emerge during the research process. This can have implications for the influence of policy networks that they belong to, policy communities and policy issues under study (Haas, 1992). Researchers are often required to provide public commentary to a variety of audiences and to be accountable to funders of the research. This may involve balancing acts that limit and enhance questions that can be asked and can serve to open or close doors on complex and dynamic policy issues.

As the analysis progresses, researchers may develop a clearer picture of how the policy may emerge and develop an interest in seeing particular policies emerging. This means that they may increasingly take up positions as stakeholders. Understood in some areas of research as the Hawthorne effect (1950) researchers who find themselves repositioning their perspectives towards those of stakeholders may unconsciously change the focus of what they are studying in efforts to secure positive change in the policy-making process.

One way to balance the flexing of positions of stakeholder researchers is to use a stakeholder analysis. This approach uses methods as tools to understand the behaviours, intentions, interrelations and interests of individuals and organisations so as to assess the influence and resources they bring to decision-making and implementation processes. Researchers who conduct stakeholder analysis are required to conduct a comprehensive analysis to produce new knowledge about policy-making processes. They have to consider all those involved or likely to be involved in the decision-making and the implications of the policy under scrutiny. Time and resources for such work may be limited, such as when the analysis is being conducted as part of a planning stage of a small local project or more wide-ranging such as when the policy is a national or international one. Policies may be about involvement of youth in local projects (e.g. Nolas, 2011) or the sale and consumption of alcohol in a country (e.g. Varvasovszky & Mckee, 1998).

Such research can be conducted by an individual but because judgement is critical, it is usually desirable to be carried out by a team in order to bring balance to both the methods employed and the assumptions and knowledge of the analysts. Given the often political nature of policy development and implementation this form of research strives to gain less individually biased perspectives of stakeholder positions and interests, by drawing on a range of qualitative and quantitative methods to reduce the imposition of untested assumptions and increase the likelihood of new directions which may be otherwise overlooked. That said, the use of a team of researchers is often dependent on financial resources available and if working as an individual researcher it is recommended that a supervisor or advisory group that includes key informants is drawn upon.

From the perspective of other stakeholders in the process the researcher stakeholder may be situated within their institutional base and their perceived legitimacy enhanced or restrained (Walt et al., 2008). The perception of researcher class, gender, caste, ethnicity and profession in addition to their perceived situatedness may directly influence how and what data is collected and interpreted. If a researcher knows that they are positioned as an insider they may feel an obligation to be biased towards the community they are working within whilst also being able to ask more meaningful questions (Merriam et al., 2001). Researchers who are positioned as outsiders may be able instead to ask taboo questions and make explicit their curiosity with the unfamiliar. In both positions the researcher may be able to elicit fuller explanations and more detail from respondents.

The construction of knowledge gained in such research can be informed by the researcher position. The research may have been constructed from the outside and based on external understandings and constructs. Outsider researchers may not have this insight whilst insiders may feel able to challenge the premise of the research study. Walt et al. (2008) counsel against overlooking the risk of superficial and decontextualised research carried out in short time frames and initiated in response to external political imperatives. They highlight that such research can lead to only part of the picture being revealed. This may also be because the researcher position can influence the choice of issues to be focused on and so in turn the research agenda and questions.

The funded researcher

Researchers may be funded to carry out research by a variety of sources. Aspiring PhD students may be awarded funding from individual universities or from national bodies such as the Economic and Social Research Council (ESRC). Postdoctoral researchers may acquire funding from local or national government, charitable bodies, national organisations, businesses and occasionally philanthropic individuals. Researchers funded to carry out doctoral studies may have relative freedom in what they research and how they conduct the research, being able to work to their own (or to their supervisor's) agenda without conforming to political or activist expectations. Often PhD researchers gaining a studentship from a university are free to use the funds in order simply to gain expertise in a particular field and make an original contribution to knowledge. Other funded researchers, however, may be funded to undertake research in order to inform policy, bring about change, raise awareness, evaluate services or highlight existing practice implications. For these researchers there can be particular challenges and sometimes constraints on how the research is conducted and to what ends.

Funded research is often conducted within a limited time frame and this can have the effect of the researcher becoming more rigid in the position that they adopt. A researcher who positions themselves as an outsider and who is then regarded as an insider by participants may close down storytelling and accounts of details of experiences in the name of completing the research on time or within budget. This clearly has an effect on the knowledge that is accessed and the research that is reported.

Funded researchers may be challenged in their positions as activists or change-makers by their funders so that the degree of change they seek to bring through the research is limited or biased. Differentials between which communities are funded and who is selected to carry out the research may exist and this, too, influences the positionality of the researcher. A researcher who is seeking to be employed and paid to conduct research may highlight to employers their value in accessing participants and may assure funders that the work will be completed on time regardless of the issues that may arise in the course of the research. If they find changes in their positionality affecting the research as it progresses they may have to negotiate the tension between meeting these assurances and attending to the challenges they face as researchers.

Funded researchers have to consider their own views on the issue under research as well as the views held by their community. If these differ to those of their funders or the community in which they are conducting the research they must find a way to recognise their positions as researchers who are perhaps less involved due to their personal beliefs.

For funded researchers working within their own communities or with other stakeholders in communities they are unfamiliar with, these challenges can be addressed by anticipating and preparing for the role that their positionality can play.

Chapter summary

This chapter has identified how positionality can be understood in all forms of research and how it may change through research processes. By examining the role of objectivity and subjectivity in researcher positionality, research that incorporates insider and outsider researcher positions, research of sensitive topics and experimental research it has shown how conscious and unconscious positions can be taken up by and imposed upon researchers. The impact of different positionalities on the research process has been considered by thinking through how personal and professional experiences can evoke challenges to the researcher position and the ways in which it can influence the research process. It has shown how emotion and affect can enter the research process.

Hints and tips

Enhancing awareness of one's positionality as a researcher enables more rigorous, reliable and trustworthy research to be carried out and for bias in its conduct and reporting to be made more explicit. In turn this allows those who read the research to have more information with which to form their own critique of it. There are a number of ways in which researchers can enhance their recognition and awareness of their positionality:

- Knowing that positionality can fluctuate throughout the research process enables you to recognise triggers for change such as accounts of experiences close to your own, beliefs and values which you may or may not be in accord with and topics that you find distressing.
- Choosing when to change your positionality can help in recognising it and can be promoted by changes in method, selecting times in the research process to reposition yourself and identifying aspects of the data that you wish to explore in more detail.
- Being aware that participants' perceptions of you will not always be obvious or what you expect them to be will enable a flexibility in how you respond to their accounts and queries.
- Maintaining field notes and reflexive journals that focus on how you felt at different parts of the research process will help you to think through the positionalities that you inhabit during the research process.

Further reading

Berger, R. (2013). Now I see it, now I don't: Researcher's position and reflexivity in qualitative research. *Qualitative Research*.

Milner IV, H. R. (2007). Race, culture, and researcher positionality: Working through dangers seen, unseen, and unforeseen. *Educational Researcher*, 36(7), 388–400.

Sherwood, S. J., Roe, C. A., Holt, N. J., & Wilson, S. (2005). Interpersonal psi – exploring the role of the experimenter and the experimental climate in a ganzfeld telepathy task. *European Journal of Parapsychology, 20*(2), 150–172.

Srivastava, P. (2006). Reconciling multiple researcher positionalities and languages in international research. *Research in Comparative and International Education*, 1(3), 210–222.

Walt, G., Shiffman, J., Schneider, H., Murray, S. F., Brugha, R., & Gilson, L. (2008). Doing health policy analysis: Methodological and conceptual reflections and challenges. *Health Policy and Planning, 239*(5), 308–317.

Researcher as instrument

3

Chapter map and outcomes

This chapter considers what the researcher *does* when they are conducting research and how this shapes the research process and its outcomes. The chapter begins by discussing what is meant by the term **research instrument** and around how this has come to include the researcher as the instrument itself. It goes on to consider the ethical issues of researchers as instrument, threats to the quality of the research brought by the researcher as instrument, biases that the researcher can bring and ways the researcher can learn to recognise biases in their research administration. The chapter concludes with hints and tips to enable researchers to better recognise themselves as research instruments, and techniques by which they can address challenges and threats to the integrity of their research brought about by their role as a research instrument.

Having read this chapter, readers will:

- Understand what a research instrument is and when they are acting as a research instrument
- Have considered what being a research instrument is and what it means for the rigour and progress of the research process
- Have identified ways to address ethical concerns arising from the researcher being a research instrument
- Have had opportunities to explore different ways in which researchers can act as instruments
- Be equipped with strategies and tips to enhance their own performance as researcher instruments.

Introduction

> **Researcher View**
>
> 'I've done work in which I am a kind of tool that's used in the research, I suppose. So the whole question of the intersubjectivity of the interviewer and interviewee becomes a theme.... I was trying to make sense of the interview in terms of things that I had or hadn't said in interview. So in order to do that I was using my subjectivity both in my experience of the interview but also as I was doing the analysis, my later interpretation of what was going on for me in the interview. So I wasn't the subject of the research, but I was using myself and my subjectivity in the research.'

In all forms of research the researcher is the person who devises the research and determines the research questions and hypotheses. They may do this alone or as part of a team. The researcher decides what to do with the data, what from the research to disseminate to a wider audience, and how to present it. As such, the researcher is instrumental in all aspects of the research. The researcher becomes the instrument when they develop research questions and hypotheses, construct and administer questions to elicit data, and test and interpret the analysis of the data. Whilst this is made explicit in qualitatively orientated research, it is often less so in quantitatively orientated research.

The objective researcher as instrument

The objective researcher recognises their role in administering the instrument, considering how their objectivity is open to compromise and recognising where they have advertently or inadvertently influenced the administration. Although there is a demand to adhere to an objective approach in experimental studies, the fact that experimental researchers devise non-standardised questions to allow them to confirm or disconfirm a particular hypothesis (Chenail, 2011) means that the objective–subjective divide is breached to some extent (Cunliffe & Karunanayake, 2013).

The subjective researcher as instrument

Whereas quantitative research commonly uses standardised and pre-tested instruments that may be questionnaires or measurement scales, the instrument of qualitative research is usually the researcher who has devised a series of open-ended questions to elicit from participants open and expansive data about the topic. In qualitative research the need for the researcher to develop a rapport with participants when in face-to-face data elicitation interactions means that their role as the research instrument is always present and can become more obvious when repeated interviews with the same participants are held (Haahr, Norlyk, & Hall, 2013). Therefore there are legitimate ethical concerns not only about the appropriateness of the questions themselves but also about the person who is asking them. The instrument by which the questions are delivered in qualitative research interviews has to be someone who is appropriately trained and supported in the construction and posing of the questions, aware of their relationship with the participants and with the research process, and also aware of their assumptions and biases about the topic they are researching.

What is a research instrument?

'Research instrument' is a generic term derived from traditional scientific research. It is applied to devices used for measurement in research. Research instruments can be either researcher-completed or participant-completed. Traditionally research instruments are developed by researchers and assessed for their **usability** (ease of use, completion and provision of interpretable data), **validity** (the extent to which the instrument measures what it is supposed to measure) and **reliability** (its consistency in measuring what it is supposed to measure).

Qualitative research regards the researcher as the instrument because when they are collecting data in face-to-face interactions with participants, the way questions are devised and presented to participants influences the response elicited by them. This means that subjective researchers need to be open to the same scrutiny and assessment as the instruments used in other forms of research.

It can be hard to determine the role of instrument in research. Objective researchers in particular may use a pre-determined questionnaire to elicit data from participants and not consider how it is administered or by whom. The questionnaire is regarded as the instrument. However, as the following research example shows, regarding questionnaires as the only instrument in research can be misleading. Considering who the researchers administering the questionnaire are can elicit more meaningful and useful data.

RESEARCH EXAMPLE

Summary of research from R. J. Moss et al. (2014). A survey of key opinion leaders to support curriculum development in advanced medical science liaison training. *Therapeutic Intervention and Regulatory Science*, 1–5.

The study: The study was conducted to develop an advanced training curriculum for experienced medical science liaisons (MSLs). MSLs are highly educated members of medical affairs departments usually located within pharmaceutical and biomedical organisations. Part of their role is to educate clinical peers about treatment guidelines, to summarise scientific congresses and to address questions of safety and efficacy. In order to gather useful information about required training for MSLs a survey was developed to identify the most highly valued skills of MSLs and those most in need of enrichment, by gathering data from 296 key opinion leaders (KOLs). The nine-question survey was developed and administered verbally at the conclusion of a routine MSL–KOL interaction by a team of MSLs drawn from diverse therapeutic areas. The survey was validated by internal medical affairs staff, and reviewed to ensure that the questions were objective and in line with regulatory compliance guidelines. MSLs used an existing customer-relationship management tool for call reporting to enter KOL responses. Participation was encouraged by specifying that data was to be analysed by total data set or therapeutic area set and not by individual MSL responses.

The results identified the top attributes, the most valued resources and key factors contributing to poor relationships between MSLs and KOLs as perceived by KOLs. KOLs advised that advanced training should include interpersonal skills, communication and networking skills and how to be an advocate for KOL needs.

Using MSLs as the instruments to conduct the survey provided them with valuable first-hand insight into the KOLs' desires, interests and preferred methods of interaction – all highlighted as key aspects of advanced training needed. Further, this approach enabled the MSLs to ask KOLs about their own effectiveness and how to become more valuable colleagues. This unique opportunity would have been lost with the use of blinded survey administrators. The MSLs reported that they gained more insight into KOLs' preferences in the first few minutes of the survey meeting than they had had in numerous previous meetings. They also mentioned that KOLs were willing to spend a few extra minutes at the conclusion of the routine interaction to answer the survey questions when they learned that their participation may result in better value being provided to them. The conduct of this survey by MSLs and the utilisation of existing data-collection technology ensured its timeliness and cost-effectiveness.

This study highlights the mutual benefits to research participants and researchers who were also practitioners, of using existing meeting times and relationships to gather data about issues that both groups had awareness of. Although this approach restricted the data-gathering opportunities and constrained who the data could be collected from, it also enabled more efficient data collection. Access to participants was facilitated, the data gathering was beneficial to both the researchers and the researched and the final outcomes of the research were useful to them and their companies. By utilising existing practitioners and relationships to gather the data, with the researchers acting as instruments of research by administering the questionnaires within known contexts and with language familiar to both groups, the respondents provided information of use to them and gained more knowledge themselves.

However, these arrangements are not always possible and researchers often find themselves collecting data using standardised questionnaires and from people that they do not have prior relationships with. For the objective researcher this places the questionnaire as the instrument and they seek to remain detached from its administration. Analysis of the data is carried out using statistical tests relevant to the data. The tests are regarded as similarly objective and the researcher is seen as playing little role in their application. However, as the next section discusses, the researcher can also be an instrument in these processes and in decisions about how to control and test for unwanted variables.

Reflective Question: What naturally occurring opportunities in your professional life could you capitalise on to gather data for research? What would be the advantages of using these opportunities? What would be the disadvantages?

Motivation in researcher-as-instrument research

Statistical research is widely considered to be objective, with the instruments of statistical tests used to ensure validity and reliability. Independent, dependent and control variables are identified and utilised to ensure that the experiment can be repeated to achieve the same results. Steps are taken to ensure that variations are recognised and eliminated as necessary and this is the purpose of **control variables**. Control variables are variables that influence the understanding of the relationship between **independent variables** and **dependent variables**. They are commonly used to capture factors that are considered extraneous to the desired effect – 'nuisance' variables. Control variables are selected according to the researcher's purpose and the context of the research design. Paradoxically, the researcher themself is seen as a 'confounding' variable in experimental research and is factored out of the analysis. However, as the next research example shows, researchers can find themselves unwittingly acting as an instrument in their choice and use of statistical tests thus potentially influencing the results in questionable ways.

RESEARCH EXAMPLE

Summary of research from W. Carlson & J. Wu (2012. The illusion of statistical control: Control variable practice in management research., Organizational Research Methods 15 (3): **413–435**

The study: The aim of the study was to explore control-variable practice in management research in relation to stated objectives for using statistical control in recommended research practice. In this study it is argued that because control variables (CVs) are weakly related to focal variables they rarely influence the interpretation of results, giving rise to conceptually ambiguous relationships, inappropriate interpretation of findings, faulty inferences and incorrect policy decisions, overall providing only an illusion that their use provides statistical control. The paper examines the ambiguity of researchers' stated purposes for using statistical control to examine whether the intents behind their use are met effectively.

The authors reviewed every article included in three respected journals in 2007 that reported results from an empirical analysis that included at least one CV in the research design. Coding for the number and type of CVs included in each study and the type of statistical analysis used were analysed. The analysis also included whether provision of a complete justification for the inclusion of each CV was included in the studies.

The paper reports that 162 studies incorporated 2864 CVs. 81 per cent provided a complete explanation of why CVs were included and descriptions of how they were measured. 8 per cent provided partial descriptions and 12 per cent provided no explanation for the inclusion of CVs. However, authors' intent behind using CVs was not well reported, with only 62 articles (38 per cent) providing some statement of the intended reason, this varying across journals.

Discussion: Against the backdrop that researchers 'worship control' (Newcombe, 2003 in Carlson & Wu, 2012) these authors argue that whilst many steps are taken to adhere to this in the research designs and choice of statistical test, with many demonstrating better reporting of CV data and justifications for its use, their use for statistical control is often not justified or

(Continued)

reported. As appropriate statistical control requires both an understanding of the intent of the control and a determination as to whether the CV inclusion achieved that control, the lack of justification creates challenges for interpreting regression coefficients. The authors suggest that researchers, and perhaps editors and reviewers, believe that the mere inclusion of CVs always brings sufficient control to improve rigour and interpretability of results. Whilst this may be true in certain circumstances, the notion that including more CVs offers a more conservative or rigorous research design can and should be challenged. Further, the authors propose that their analysis found that few CVs included in designs appear to have any substantive impact on results.

This paper suggests that decisions about the inclusion of CVs in research designs may be more to placate future reviewers than to enhance the meaning of findings. Many CVs included have no impact on research design and if they do the mismatch of current practice to statistical control practice is more likely to confound than to clarify research findings. The authors conclude that the skilful use of these tools by researchers is a responsibility that overarches the intent behind their use and that without this researchers may be better served to leave CVs out of research design.

Although focused on the use of statistical tests and measures, the study shows the need for the researcher to regard themselves as an instrument that determines the practice and outcome of the research. In this instance they are instruments that must responsibly decide on what tests to use and introduce and what this will bring to the study. Their motivation for the use of tests must go beyond being seen to bring control and towards justifying and achieving the desired control.

This rationale is key to the subjective researcher as instrument who needs not only to decide what instrument they will use to gather and analyse data but also very often to develop that instrument. This means that the subjective researcher moves beyond being an instrument who selects and applies a data-gathering and analysis technique, to becoming part of the process. The objective stance is rejected in favour of a subjective one that recognises the motivation and knowledge of the researcher alongside their decision to use the chosen technique.

Researcher as instrument in interviews

One of the most common data-gathering techniques in qualitative research is the semi-structured interview. This requires an interview schedule consisting of a few guide questions to be devised in advance of the interview. The questions are always open and seeking to enable the participants to speak freely of what is significant to them. The questions may not always be used in the same order, not all will necessarily be used, and there is scope to use probe questions to obtain further detail in the course of the interview.

In addition to devising an interview schedule, subjective researchers have to recognise the relevance of the research settings, relationships and contexts, and see their own role in generating accounts from respondents as key. This places responsibility on the researcher to justify not only their choice of the interview as the data-gathering technique but also the way in which the interview is conducted. In turn this requires researchers conducting interviews to consider the assumptions based on pre-existing knowledge they are bringing to the interview and its questions, as well as personal characteristics they have which may influence how the interview is conducted, how the questions are put to interviewees and how personal interactions may influence the responses. Whilst this calls for personal reflexive awareness by researchers of themselves, their role and the methods they are bringing to the research, this approach also offers the possibility of inquiring in a way that is guided by the respondent. In order to facilitate this a number of protocols and guidelines about non-standardised interviews have been developed. They provide ways of developing the questions and their probes, of considering the presentation of these questions in the interviews and of following them up in line with the directions that the participants take the interviews. These protocols aim to ensure that whilst primarily led by participants, the researcher acts as the instrument who elicits information pertinent to the topic of interest in ways that allow for events and experiences of significance to the participants to be spoken about. The role of the researcher instrument, whilst guided by these protocols, also relies on their capacity for effective communication and interaction with the participant. As an experienced researcher describes in the extract below, this can be as challenging as developing the questions:

Researcher View

'I suddenly became aware that I had failed to follow the methodology of this method, which suggested, required me, to follow up on things that the participant had said in an initial answer to a big open-ended question. And she'd talked quite a lot in her initial narrative about having been married against her will when she was 17... and I then didn't follow that up and ask her anything about it, even though she'd said quite a lot about it initially, and that was against the protocol of the interview. It was almost a sabotage of the interview process.

'...and here I was being offered by an interviewee an opportunity to talk about that [arranged marriages versus forced marriages] and I just didn't do it. I didn't pick it up, I didn't ask her anymore about it. I left it alone.

'Once I realised this had happened, it was like well why did I do this? So actually a lot of the paper then ends up being about why did I fail to follow the protocols of this interview, what was going on for me, because the interview really relied on me doing certain things and I didn't do them. So what was that about and was that about my kind of, was it some kind of political enactment of mine of saying I'm not going to try and make this woman represent all women of that culture? And you know was it a kind of feminist political counter act against the way we'd set up the research, or was it – I think there may be an element of that – but I also end up unpacking a whole set of things to do with the interviewee's relationship with her mother and my relationship with my mother.

'...and I then relate that to my experience at that time which was my mother was very sick and dying when I was doing the interview and my own history with my mother was quite a difficult relationship that had been reconciled and I wanted to protect that. And in a sense I started to understand what I had done in this interview as being both about the kind of bigger politics of the interview and of the way that we might set up, you know one person to try and represent a set of issues. But also about what that tells us about the importance of kind of a reparative relationship between mother and daughter and how that can help us understand, particularly her relationship, the relationship she had to both living in London and overseas. It's a complicated argument, quite a complex argument, but it was one that really relied on a moment of revelation about some of the parallels between my life and the interviewee's life, even though ostensibly there was a cultural chasm between us, we had very different lives. But actually there was some shared experience around a fractured relationship with our mothers that was repaired and my recognition of how precious that was, it was also about my sadness about my mother who was dying. Well maybe actually she had just died at that point when I did the interview. It was certainly very alive for me.'

This very personal account of a researcher's in-depth consideration of her role as an instrument on which the research relied shows how she considered wider political concerns, cultural differences and commonalities in personal relationships to understand what had prevented her from conducting an interview that accurately followed the interview protocols. It highlights the impact of this on the choice of data elicitation, the data gathering and its later analysis. The researcher's subsequent decision to write up this experience into a published paper shows, too, how valuing the researcher as instrument can lead to new understanding of the self as a researcher instrument and of how it can influence the quality of the research.

Reflective Question: Researchers gather information in many ways, in addition to asking people about themselves. What other ways can you think of and what is your role as an instrument for data collection? Think about how experience can be expressed visually, pictorially and through performance.

Sometimes, semi-structured interviews are designed not only to ask questions about a topic but also to access unlooked-for information about a participant's experience and understanding and to consider what is not said as much as what participants choose to say in a collaborative exchange between the interviewer and the research participant. This facilitative interaction sets up a 'conversational space' in which the interviewer aims to develop an 'arena of topics, gestures and languages safely available to individuals in a given arena' (Owens, 2006, p. 1161).

The conversational space

The conversational space is important in recognising that the narration of experiences is the creation of public identities. Narrators choose how to present themselves to others by selecting from available resources in language and common discourse. They usually want to do so in a convincing and acceptable way (Owens, 2006). The role of the interviewer becomes a collaborative one in which the ways in which stories are told and heard are determined not only by how they are narrated but also by how they are listened and responded to. For the researcher as instrument this can mean using 'their sensory organs to grasp the study object, mirroring them in their consciousness, where they can then be converted into phenomenological representations to be interpreted' (Turato, 2005, p. 510) but the ways in which this can be done vary.

Researchers have to be careful not to create a superficial form of friendship or to distance themselves from the interviewee through self-disclosure that may only highlight differences in personal experience

(Frost & Holt, 2014), in the belief that displaying empathy to establish rapport with the interviewee is always interpreted by them as mutual understanding. Training and practice in carrying out semi-structured interviews can go someway to helping interviewers become effective but as the following study shows, some researcher attributes and practices can be more effective than others.

RESEARCH EXAMPLE

Summary of research from A. Pezalla, J. Pettigrew M., & Miller-Day (2012). Researching the researcher-as-instrument: An exercise in self-reflexivity. *Qualitative Research, 12*(2), 165–185.

Aim: To understand how researchers as instruments facilitate unique conversational spaces in research interviews and to determine if there are researcher attributes or practices that are more effective than others in eliciting detailed narratives from respondents. This study focuses on the embodiment of the researcher conducting interviews to explore the unique attributes brought by them to the practice of the interview.

Methodology: Interviewers were given four hours of training in which they reviewed interview protocol and procedure, summarised guidelines for ethical research and practised carrying out interviews. Each was given an Interview Schedule and instructed to use it only as a guide, posing the questions in their own words to respondents and using additional questions and probes as necessary.

The interviews were conducted individually with adolescents within a school setting. They aimed to understand the social context of substance use for rural adolescents living in two Mid-Atlantic States of the US. The interviews ranged in duration from 18 to 91 minutes and were digitally recorded.

Analysis: Three of the interviewers adopted an explicit self-reflexive stance in which they agreed that it was necessary to 'understand ourselves as part of the process of understanding others' (Ellis & Berger, 2003, p. 486). They began the analysis by discussing amongst themselves the risks of self-reflexively examining their own work, which they acknowledged as the most difficult step of the analysis process. They restricted their analysis to three selected topics (rural living, identity and future selves, and risky behaviour). The topics were chosen to represent different levels of emotional risk for the respondents, as well as a cross-section of the wider foci of the study.

Each related passage in the interview transcripts was identified by each researcher using the same iterative analysis process that consisted of analysis of their own individual transcripts followed by a cross-analysis of each other's transcripts. Interviewer practice was defined as an action performed repeatedly and categorised into groups of interviewer characteristics. Interviewer characteristics were defined as a distinguishing general feature or overall quality of the interviewer.

Throughout the process each researcher developed and refined their code lists and held weekly discussions with each other to discuss them. Each then re-coded a portion of each other's transcripts and calculated the percentage of raw coding agreement. Disagreements were negotiated until consensus on a working list of codes of at least 80 per cent was reached.

Finally, the code list was reduced to a common set of researcher-as-instrument characteristics and interviewing practices.

Findings: Interviewer Characteristics: One interviewer's (Annie) characteristics were coded as 'affirming', 'energetic' and 'interpretive' based on her use of phrases such as 'that's so cool, that's great' and 'showing wonder, astonishment, or confusion by something the respondent said that was unexpected or remarkable' (p. 171). 'Interpretive' was defined as 'expressing a personal opinion or interpretation regarding something respondent said' (p. 172).

Another interviewer's (Jonathan) characteristics were neutrality ('not engaged on one side of argument or another, neither affirming nor disapproving of respondent stories') and naivety ('showing a lack of knowledge or information about the respondent'). This interviewer was summarised as making shorter utterances and fewer opinionated responses than Annie.

The third interviewer's (Michelle) characteristics were coded as being higher in affirmation ('showing support for a respondent's idea or belief') and self-disclosure than either Annie or Jonathan. The transcripts were filled with encouragement and compliments towards her respondents and she used stories of her own adolescent son to explain a topic she wanted to discuss with the respondent.

These instrument qualities were found in nearly every topic of discussion for each interviewer, although all showed other qualities at different points of the interviews. The characteristics defined above functioned differently across the different conversation topics. The variance in interviewer characteristics did not appear to have much impact on the quality of responses elicited about low-risk topics (rural living). When talking about moderately risky topics (identity and future selves) the neutrality characteristic appeared effective in facilitating an open conversational space, whilst the affirming characteristic offered a more nurturing environment for conversation. The high-risk topic (alcohol and drug use) seemed to be least affected by the interpretive approach, also appearing to inhibit responses, whilst the neutrality and self-disclosing characteristics elicited the most detailed narratives.

Conclusions: The researchers highlight that the interviewing styles were rooted in traditional gender norms that included minimalist and neutral stereotypical masculine norms (Jonathan) through to effusive and affirming,

(Continued)

traditionally feminine norms (Annie and Michelle). This raises the question of the role of gender in influencing conversational spaces in interviews and suggests that qualities cannot be disentangled. Reflexive practice should therefore acknowledge not only what an interviewer says and how it is said but also the ways in which utterances are connected to the interviewer's gender.

Despite the training that each of the researchers had undergone prior to carrying out the interviews in this study, their personal characteristics along with the common mistakes of asking overlong or closed questions led them to conclude not only that researchers are the instruments in qualitative interview research but also that they are 'differently calibrated instruments' (p. 182).

This study highlights the role of personal characteristics in affecting the function and effectiveness of the researcher as instrument. These authors are amongst many that highlight the dynamic nature of qualitative interviews and the multiple identities inhabited by those carrying them out. They show that personal characteristics and interviewer styles influence the data collection and the facilitation of the interview. Some of these are in the control of the interviewer but others can be attributed to fixed dimensions such as gender.

The role of gender in interviews has been discussed by researchers such as Catherine Kohler Riessman. Riessman suggests that although important it is not always enough to consider and assume that women interviewing women ensures an appropriate conversational space. She describes interviews by women with other women about marital separation (Riessman, 1987) in which the temporal nature of the narrations provided by white middle-class American women resonated with the white middle-class American interviewer but that the episodic narration of the working-class Puerto Rican women presented challenges to the interviewer so that she missed key themes and inhibited the narrative flow of the interview. It was only in revisiting the interview transcript that she was able to identify these issues, attributed by her to cultural differences, as highlighting the necessity for interviewers to challenge taken-for-granted assumptions about gender–gender communication. Riessman suggests that researchers work instead to retain the wholeness of narrations in order to look beyond 'cleaned-up' speech for features of speech that may provide further insight into the meanings in the narratives. Examples of features of speech may be repetition and the return to particular topics or the use of metaphors to indicate emotions that cannot be otherwise verbalised.

As well as recognising personal characteristics that can enhance the development of rapport and a useful conversational space, it is also important to recognise personal characteristics that can knowingly inhibit the researcher-as-instrument role. Recognising that personal characteristics and performance can influence the development and maintenance of rapport during interviews or other face-to-face research interactions can be fruitful in helping researchers to prepare to conduct research and anticipate challenges and problems in carrying it out. Prepared in this way, researchers can develop and bring with them to the research interaction strategies for negotiating and addressing such challenges. However, the research setting and expectations can also lead to the emergence of identities and personal characteristics that can inhibit the research encounter. These may be accounted for to some extent by essential unchangeable characteristics that inform ways of communicating for individual researchers but may also be transient constructions that emerge unexpectedly in the research process. Whilst the 'ideal researcher' may be one whose skills are unaffected by the research context, is assertive in negotiating access and developing rapport and is comfortable in presenting themselves as competent in method and communication, the converse of this is the 'reluctant' or 'shy' researcher (Scott, Hinton-Smith, Härmä, & Broome, 2012).

Reflective Question: What is it about you that will aid and hinder data collection? Will this be different with different groups of participants?

The reluctant researcher

Researcher characteristics can emerge due to the pressures of the research environment, self-doubt about one's ability to conduct the research, an inclination towards nervousness, or stress about managing feelings evoked in carrying out the research. Scott et al. (2012) point out that both the 'ideal' researcher and the 'reluctant' researcher can be understood as performances in situational roles into which any individual can drift. The emotion work needed to play down tendencies towards embarrassment or nervousness by the researcher and to play up the appearance of a confident and socially assertive researcher can be as demanding and influential to the research as looking for and working with these characteristics in the participant.

The following research study led to the development of a 'cringe spectrum' by Scott et al. (2012, p. 721), and is useful in identifying the different situations within the research process that can evoke self-conscious emotions of shame, embarrassment and shyness for researchers.

RESEARCH EXAMPLE

Summary of research from S. Scott et al. (2012). The reluctant researcher: Shyness in the field. *Qualitative Research*, 12(6), 715–734.

The study formed part of a larger project, 'Supporting Shy Users in Pervasive Computing' (funded by the EPSRC) and focused on research conducted in a small regional contemporary art gallery, and a large traditional museum. Both settings were housing exhibitions of digital interactive art. The studies involved gathering qualitative observational field notes, visitor tracking maps, self-completion visitor questionnaires, emotion maps and visitor interviews conducted face-to-face, by email, by telephone and by walking around with the participants ('walkaround interviews', Ross, 2009). Perspectives of gallery curators, digital interactive artists, teachers and others working on community-based arts project were also gathered using workshops, interviews and focus groups. The researchers had self-identified themselves as shy to varying degrees and used reflective discussions between themselves to explore the experience of undertaking data-collection. The findings of the study found that for each individual, self-conscious emotions of shame, embarrassment or shyness were evoked by real or anticipated loss of face, compromised role performance and interactional strain according to the differing levels of face-to-face interaction required by the research.

The study led to the development of the 'cringe spectrum' of self-consciousness which consisted of four points. The first and lowest point was identified during the phase of preparing and setting up the project; the usual activities of literature searches, identifying research locations and participant access using the web and other administrative tasks conducted from the desk allowed for rehearsal and change in the privacy of the office. The next point arose when moving into the field but with relatively indirect face-to-face interaction such as covert observations and scoping of the research location (in this case a public art gallery and a museum). The third point came when some interaction with participants was required such as email correspondence, telephone interviews and focus groups. The pre-arranged agendas and explicit professional roles of these interactions provided some protection and security for the researchers. This was compromised when researchers were required to interact in real-life situations, sometimes by spontaneously approaching participants to request interviews or survey completion, and having to adapt to the unpredictability of live face-to-face interaction, making this the highest and fourth point on the cringe spectrum. The stress that arose from these types of situations was caused by anticipation of embarrassment from 'negative social reactions, awkward mismatches of perceived intentions and subsequent losses of internal scripts' (Gross & Stone, 1964) that threatened to evoke feelings of shame and discreditation of intended impressions (Scott et al., 2012, p. 722). Conversely, these researchers were also concerned about appearing too competent, risking creating a distance from potential participants that would threaten the rapport sought through establishing equal status.

Management of emotions by researchers in their role is a complex process that aims both to maintain a professional appearance and to safeguard participants' welfare. When conducting research in unfamiliar settings and social environments, feelings of incompetence and fear of exposure and embarrassment can give rise to shyness. To manage this, researchers have to employ emotional labour to reconcile the tension between managing their private selves and the impressions they give to others. The sensations arising for the researchers in the study were found to be heightened by those who define themselves as shy people but can also be drifted into by non-shy individuals under conditions that provoke them.

> **Reflective Question:** Where would you be in the cringe spectrum at the different stages of the research described above?

Emotional labour

Whilst personal characteristics such as gender may be beyond personal control, the example above shows that the influence of emotions on the identity created in the research process may not be. Counsellors and other healthcare providers are often trained in ways to hide personal upset or distress when working with clients who have experienced distressing incidents in order to maintain the focus on them and their recounting of experiences. The importance of masking emotions lies in the need not to appear overwhelmed or distressed by what is being recounted so that the narrator feels able to continue to talk about personal issues in the quest to understand and find solutions in ways of dealing with them. Many research studies focus on sensitive or distressing topics, and whilst ethical considerations go some way to ensuring the protection of the participants from further distress being caused to them by participation in the research study, there is also a need to pay attention to the care of the researcher who is the instrument by which the sensitive research is being conducted.

Hochschild (2003) identified the presence of emotional labour in service industries, defining it as that which 'requires one to induce or suppress feeling in order to sustain the outward countenance that produces the proper state of mind in others' (p. 7). She defined two key forms of emotional labour: surface acting, in which the emotions that are not felt are enacted and 'deep acting', in which feelings that are induced are actively supressed so as to be inaccessible both to the agent and to the public. The importance of emotional labour is seen to lie in its recognition as a key characteristic of jobs requiring interaction with the public but also as a source of burn-out and stress for those undertaking them (e.g. Lings, Durden, Lee, & Cadogan, 2010).

Hochschild's study was carried out in relation to service industries and concluded that it may be beneficial to develop an emotional detachment from customers and clients in order to maintain beneficial contact between the worker and the public. In seeking to develop rapport with a research participant, however, as a researcher seeks to do, the self-protection afforded by psychological distancing from participants or data can obscure and inhibit the recounting and illuminations of meanings by and within them, risking the data losing meaning or the participant not feeling able to recount what is of significance to them. Furthermore, researchers may feel distressed at having to display an emotional absence at times when they are experiencing intense emotions in response to hearing of participants' distress. On the other hand, it is argued that overextension of emotion in the experiences of others can lead to 'a feeling of compulsion to reflect on aspects of their own lives, or to re-evaluate painful memories' (Harris & Ogbonna, 2012, p. 549), and can inhibit rapport and flow in the interview and interpretation phases of the interview.

RESEARCH EXAMPLE

Summary of research from E. Ogbonna & L. C. Harris (2004). Work intensification and emotional labour amongst UK university lecturers: An exploratory study. *Organizational Studies, 25,* 1185–1203.

Lecturers at UK universities were interviewed to assess the frequency and propensity of emotional labour and the extent to which emotional labour is becoming part of their work. The role of intensifying changes to the work environment of UK university lecturers was examined to understand how emotional labour is derived from this, and the positive and negative emotional consequences of work intensification and emotional labour considered. The study found that pressures arising from issues such as the greater commercialisation of universities leading to increased numbers of students without associated increased funding have increased organisational expectations placed on lecturers. In turn this has led to an association of emotional labour with 'professionalism'. Positive consequences included the development of effective coping strategies by using surface acting and a professional detachment from having to care about every single student. Related to this was reward in the form of career progression for those lecturers who demonstrated the ability to display 'appropriate' behaviours and emotions. However, negative outcomes were also reported. These included feelings of inadequacy amongst lecturers at having to 'fake' emotions in order to comply with apparently legitimate institutional demands, often leading to high levels of stress. Interaction between colleagues was also affected, as lecturers feared showing signs of weakness in coping to colleagues, when in the past they may have sought informal support from them. Competition between colleagues and the associated sense of isolation added to this, despite all those interviewed suggesting that they knew that everyone was emotionally labouring as part of the job.

The notion of emotional labour becoming part of the job is one that becomes relevant to researcher interviewers and, arguably, particularly so for those conducting sensitive research. Sensitive research is defined as more than simply considering the impact of 'taboo' topics with participants and instead considers what may be intrusive (Sampson, Bloor & Fincham, 2008, in Harris & Ogbonna, 2012) and that which imposes a substantial threat to those who are or have been involved in it (Dickson-Swift, James & Liamputtong, 2008 in Harris and Ogbonna, 2012). Importantly, sensitive research includes all those involved in it and goes beyond considering only the participants, to remember the researchers, interviewers, transcribers and participants (Malacrida, 2007 in Ogbonna & Harris, 2012). For all, the implication of 'substantial threat' is that sensitive research may incur costs for any party (Johnson & Mcleod Clarke, 2003). The following example illustrates some of the cost to researchers and the impact on researchers when collecting sensitive data.

RESEARCH EXAMPLE

Summary of research from B. Johnson & J. Macleod Clarke (2003). Collecting sensitive data: The impact on researchers. *Qualitative Health Research*, *13*, 421–434.

The study aimed to investigate the experiences of collecting sensitive data of researchers who had conducted recent studies on HIV/AIDS, dying and death. Researchers were invited to reflect on the study in which they were or had been engaged during one-to-one recorded interviews. They were asked to describe the nature of the study and also their experiences and any concerns or issues they had encountered during the research process. All researchers described finding the data-collection process stressful. Common issues and concerns were identified as: inexperience and lack of training, confidentiality, role conflict, impact of interviews on participants and feelings of isolation.

   (i)   Inexperience and lack of training: issues raised included contact anxiety, confronting and dealing with anxiety and working in uncharted territory. These arose principally from feeling that the preparation for the in-depth interviews had focused overly on assessing participants and data analysis and with little or no consideration for the kinds of difficulties and concerns researchers may encounter during the research process. This was particularly relevant to interviewing participants in their own homes.

   (ii)   Concerns about confidentiality: issues raised included fear of participants being identified when reporting study findings, including by family members, and pressure to 'report back' to health professionals. These were of particular concern when the location of the study could be easily identified.

  (iii)   Role conflict: this arose for those researchers who were also healthcare practitioners, particularly when they found that participants had been misinformed or had misunderstood information given to them about their condition. The researchers used strategies of explaining potential sources of help and information and in some cases arranged for the participant to discuss their concerns with an appropriate healthcare practitioner. There were instances, however, when participants did not express concern and the researchers were left wondering whether to break confidentiality in the interests of the participant's welfare. This concern sometimes lasted long after the completion of the study. Role conflict also led to feelings of guilt at not being able to provide help to the participant because of their researcher role.

Some researchers also spoke of conflict between their role as a friend and as a data collector, particularly when trying to establish an empathic rapport. They expressed concern at almost losing sight of their professional role when feeling the need to behave as a friend, particularly so when the participant was dying or very ill. Others were concerned that because of these conflicts they had influenced the course of the interview.

(iv) Impact of the interview on the participants: the researchers expressed concern that they could never be certain that some of the participants had not been harmed by the experience of telling their stories in the research interviews. They drew clear lines between counselling, in which clients express a need to be interviewed, and research interviews, in which potential participants are approached and invited (or, as some researchers felt, coerced) to be interviewed.

(v) Isolation: several researchers felt unsupported and isolated during the data-collection phases of the research. They felt a need for supervision and also to separate home and work. Often finding that the only support available to them was from friends and family, they also felt a reluctance to take the distress home or to inflict it on those close to them. Geographical distance between the research field and the research institution inhibited access to supervisors and team meetings tended to focus on the research process rather than personal issues. There was also concern that expressing personal impact could be perceived as weakness or deficit in themselves as researchers.

This study illustrates the need for better preparation by and for researchers conducting sensitive research, particularly when the emotional content is related to real-life experiences with which researchers might readily identify. Training should include focus on negotiating access, interviewing skills and the role relationship with participants. It should include strategies that help to deal with potential difficulties and concerns arising from the data-collection process and adequate supervision and support for the researchers should be built into the research design. The professional background of the researcher should be considered for its potential impact on the data-collection process and the personal challenges of overriding this role during the research process anticipated. It may also be important to consider the age and experience of researchers to consider how they may react and respond to interview situations, as well as whether this has influence on the degree of sensitisation to the needs of the participants.

Reflective Question: What topics would you be sensitive about researching? Think about why this would be. Is it because of personal experience or because of concern for participants describing their experiences to you?

Negotiating risk

The conundrum facing both narrator and listener in the interview setting is that whilst both recognise that some decisions and experiences are acceptable and sanctioned by social expectations, others are not, and researchers seek to delve into the private worlds of both. One example is motherhood, a status that is laden with cultural expectations of instinct and pleasure. There are many ways of telling every story and the language and justification used may vary with the person it is being told to. In the research interview the interviewer is required to find ways to enhance the co-authorship of the story by developing a safe conversational space in which a significant story may be told in a way that acknowledges that shame and embarrassment may be present but does not prevent the story being told more easily and protects the narrator's public identity formed through its telling. This may mean recognising the use of metaphor as a way of negotiating the boundary between topic and language (Lakoff & Johnson, 1980).

Metaphors are a figurative use of language, which at their simplest are 'devices of representation through which new meaning may be learned' (Coffey & Atkinson, 1996). They can be regarded as linguistic devices that describe 'understanding and experiencing one kind of thing in terms of another' (Lakoff & Johnson, 1980). Metaphors serve a particular purpose for the speaker. They are grounded in socially shared knowledge and conventional usage, which means that metaphorical statements reveal shared cultural and social understandings of knowledge. Metaphors have been compared to dreams in the collaboration required between dreamer and waker (narrator and listener) for their interpretations (Davidson, 1979). This comparison enables interpretations of their meaning within texts as reactive endeavours that are little guided by rules (Davidson, 1979). In research interviews they can be recognised as a way of expanding conversational space to breach the topic/language boundary or of limiting it if the breach is considered inappropriate by either narrator or teller.

RESEARCH EXAMPLE

Summary of research from N. A. Frost (2009). 'Do you know what I mean?': The use of a pluralistic narrative analysis interpretation of an interview. *Qualitative Research*, 9(1), 9–29.

In a study of women making the transition to second-time motherhood (Frost, 2006), one woman used metaphors such as 'like a tidal wave' and 'car crash' in accounts of becoming a first-time mother. Recognising this as most often being coupled with descriptions of herself as a 'control freak' enabled the researcher to understand that whilst this woman expected to lose control over some of the practical changes in her life that having a baby would bring, she had been unprepared for the overwhelming of her emotions and the impact this had on her when she entered motherhood. Rather than telling the interviewer that her new status as a mother had been difficult and hard on the reformulation of her identity, the narrator and the teller were able to co-construct a story of emotional challenge with the use of metaphors.

Researchers and silence

In a book of collected readings about secrecy and silence in the research process – *Secrecy and Silence in the Research Process: Feminist reflections* by Róisín Ryan-Flood & Rosalind Gill (2010) – the responsibility of researchers not to represent as commonplace that which is not, to respect that there may be essential reasons for secrecy and silence, and that the silences and secrets can be the researcher's as much as the participant's, form key arguments. Silence can be an important part of identity or survival for participants such as those who choose to remain silent about their sexuality in restrictive societies (e.g. Parpart, in Ryan-Flood & Gill, 2010). Similarly, choices about whether to remain silent about issues such as female circumcision challenge researchers with questions about their role in apparently condoning practices they disagree with (e.g. Moore in Ryan-Flood & Gill, 2010). The book questions not the process of giving of voice that feminist research sets out to address but the moments of secrecy and silence that accompany this. It places emphasis on ensuring that whilst voices are heard in feminist research such moments are not overlooked. The book includes less-considered topics such as the role of the researcher's body in research, for example in research about obesity and dieting (Gimlin & Throsby, 2010 in Ryan-Flood & Gill, 2010), and dilemmas of 'crossing the line' when conducting covert research, for example as a female 'door supervisor' at a nightclub (O'Brien, 2010 in Ryan-Flood & Gill, 2010).

When researchers are the instrument of the research it can be challenging to remain silent in the face of distressing, controversial or contentious accounts being provided by participants. The readings in the book illustrate how silence by researchers can lead to researchers' discomfort but that silence by participants can also be necessary for them. It is the challenging task of the researcher instrument to attempt to discern the meanings and reasons for silences, both on their own part and on the part of participants. With this comes risks: risks that the breaking of the silence will threaten the participants' well-being and risks that researchers will interpret silence in ways that are not intended by the participants. There is risk for researchers who use themselves as instruments to gain understanding of the private lives of others whilst also maintaining concern for participant welfare. Many subjective researchers, particularly feminist subjective researchers, will additionally seek emancipation for research participants whose voices and lives have been marginalised, oppressed or obscured, both during the research and as a result of it. Whilst such ethical and personal considerations are important to the research, to its aims and to the usefulness of its outcomes, there can be a high cost to the researchers carrying it out (Sampson, Bloor, & Fincham, 2008).

To understand some of these costs it is useful to briefly consider why and how researchers place themselves at such risks. Feminist research has done much to advocate and develop research techniques that minimise the distance between the researcher and the researched. It calls for greater consciousness of power relationships in research and for ways to flatten such hierarchies in research relationships. Feminist research argues for more sensitivity about how knowledge is created, who it is accessible to and how it is identified. Feminist researchers are called upon to consider their own role in the research by adopting reflexive practices in which their motivations and aims for the research, alongside their personal assumptions and biases, are brought to it and regarded as part of the research process. There is no single approach to feminist methodology and no single epistemology. Whilst often associated with the rise of qualitative methodology, it has been argued that quantitative research methods also have a role to play in feminist research, either through mixed approaches, such as qualitatively driven mixed-methods research, which enable women's descriptions of issues important to them to be central to the research (e.g. Hesse-Biber, 2010) or as standalone approaches that adopt strong objectivity. Thus feminist researchers can adopt epistemologies that can range from social constructionist to critical realist to positivist.

Researching women's lives from a feminist perspective, Maynard argues that quantification has been identified with positivism and with that comes assumed imposition of standardised variables about how people live their lives, which distort rather than reflect the meanings of experiences and seek to separate the researcher from the research process (Maynard, 1994). Feminist approaches to positivism, however, enable the researcher to be an instrument within this paradigm, too.

Reflective Question: How easy is it for you to remain silent? What provokes you to speak up? How often do you stay silent even when you want to say something?

When feminist approaches were emerging it was in response to the absence of acknowledgement of women's lives as different to those of men. Dominant research of the time was based on the premise that researchers were already sufficiently familiar with the phenomenon being investigated to be able to specify in advance how to encapsulate, categorise and measure the full range of experiences. It was therefore neither exploratory nor investigatory in relation to the lives of women (Maynard, 1994). Feminists argue that there are aspects to women's lives that cannot be pre-known or pre-defined in such ways. As qualitative approaches allow for the generation of knowledge derived intersubjectively and situated in the context of how it is generated and who is using it, feminist research came to be dominated by qualitative research approaches. With this, a perceived antipathy to quantitative approaches as being useful to advancing understanding of women's lives arose, as the assumption was that it was only through qualitative methods, and especially the in-depth qualitative interview method, that useful knowledge could be generated.

However, feminism also recognises that there is a need for a measure by which to judge knowledge (Westmarland, 2001). Suggested measures have included the effect that the research has on improving women's lives (Reinharz, 1983), its potential to orient research practice toward progressive emancipation and humanisation (Mies, 1983) and subjective experience as an index of research adequacy (Dubois, 1983).

There are practical considerations to objective research that can address the apparent lack of subjectivity in it. Several researchers (e.g. Graham, 1983; Kelly, Regan & Burton, 1992) have pointed out that ways in which survey questions are framed can perpetuate the notion that men and women are equal units for measurement. Language used plays a key role, along with the issues that are asked about. A researcher devising questions for use in surveys can consider alternative language as well as questions that have not been previously asked (and, perhaps, why this may be).

RESEARCH EXAMPLE

Summary of research from N. Westmarland & J. Anderson (2001). Safe at the wheel? Security issues for female taxi drivers: Visions of a feminine future. *The Security Journal*, 14(2), 29–40.

This study aimed to investigate the prevalence of violence against male and female taxi drivers. To discover the prevalence of sexual abuse, questions were framed using the term 'sexual harassment' instead of 'sexual abuse' because 'abuse' is a term more commonly used to describe abuse against children (despite the researcher's personal view that abuse and harassment are the same experience). The question was constructed as 'Have you ever experienced sexual harassment at work?' Data gathered showed that male taxi drivers are sexually harassed at work, although to a lesser extent than female taxi drivers.

The researcher points out that the question about sexual abuse/harassment had not been asked in previous surveys about violence towards taxi drivers. This carries a supposition that the issue does not affect the population in which the research is being conducted. The ensuing lack of research into it serves to perpetuate such incorrect assumptions.

In addition to researchers considering how they are asking questions and what questions they are asking, the focus of research is also within their gift as instruments. Researchers using quantitative methods have made important political contributions by enumerating issues such as the incidence and severity of domestic violence risks, financial and promotion inequality for women in the workplace and the feminisation of poverty (Maynard, 1994). The polarisation of qualitative and quantitative methods is not beneficial to research in general and the claiming of qualitative research as being the only form of feminist research because it is the only way in which researchers can subjectively influence research is incorrect. Traditional quantitative methods can incorporate researcher subjectivity and place a greater emphasis on the role of the researcher as instrument, as the above examples have illustrated.

To conclude, this chapter discusses ways in which methods and strategies can be brought by researchers to the research process in order to aid their role and identify challenges to it as an instrument of the research. The next section on deliberative research considers how the researcher can manage value-laden research using a systematic approach that also allows for subjective insight from themselves and the participants. The chapter then goes on to consider how researchers as instruments of data interpretation can approach the task in different ways.

Deliberative research

Deliberative research acknowledges the researcher role in making value-laden decisions when conducting research into issues such as poverty and well-being and quality of life (Burchardt, 2014). It recognises researchers' roles in determining notions of adequacy and quality and that developing research around these topics can require arbitrary or scientific justification about which researchers may feel uncomfortable or embarrassed. The impact on the research can threaten its quality and its outcomes. Deliberative research aims to overcome these risks by eliciting views and value judgements from the general public in order to support or otherwise absolve the researcher from the responsibility. It aims to gather normative conclusions not reachable by common in-depth research techniques such as interviewing. Deliberative research is used across topics relevant to policy-making, public engagement and social research and has emerged from roots in the 'deliberative turn' within democratic theory that emphasises citizen participation in debate as essential to ensuring better informed and contrasting points of view (Weinstock & Kahane, 2010 in Burchardt, 2014, p. 355). To be regarded as deliberative, the participation must include debate between diverse groups and the inclusion of external evidence and information. This is practised, for example, through the development of citizens' juries run by government think tanks or the inclusion of neighbourhood considerations on city-wide budgets (e.g. Baiocchi, 2003). However, when the deliberative exercise is not tied, or at least only loosely tied, to governmental and policy-making processes it is regarded by some as research, such as in deliberative workshops, polls and focus groups. Deliberative exercises thus have a range of purposes but their separateness from democratic decision-making means that deliberation as research is currently under-theorised (Burchardt, 2014).

One team of researchers who are addressing this have identified the potential for participation by a broader range of people, through the development of short-term approaches to deliberative research (Branney, Strickland, Darby, White, & Jain, 2016). Recognising that the long-term commitment required to take part in research as part of an advisory or steering group can risk limiting the participation of the service users or other 'expert participants' who take part to those from a narrow socio-economic background (and often one similar to that of the researchers themselves), Branney et al. (2016) have designed participation based on three principles of autonomy and rationality, time limited and rapport building.

RESEARCH EXAMPLE

Summary of research from P. Branney, C. Strickland, F. Darby, L. White & S. Jain (forthcoming). Health psychology research using participative mixed qualitative methods and framework analysis: Exploring men's experiences of diagnosis and treatment for prostate cancer in Brooks, J. & King, N. (Eds) (2016) *Applied Qualitative Research in Psychology,* Palgrave: London

To incorporate a wide range of autonomous decision-making that is based both on individual (personal) autonomy and on structural (cultural and service-based) autonomy, a one-day workshop was held in order to attract a range of people to include those that may be put off by a long-term commitment to participation. The workshop aimed to elicit information about the experience of choosing treatment for low- or medium-risk prostate cancer. Participants were drawn from a group of stakeholders that included those diagnosed, those providing medical care, those managing medical care provision and researchers who would go on to collect further data in a subsequent series of focus groups. This approach served not only to involve as wide a range of participants as possible but also to incorporate knowledge-building about research methods, treatment choices and wider cultural and health services contexts in an environment in which efforts are made to include all views and ideas on an equal basis so that the 'story' and outcomes of the research represented all those taking part. Together the participants designed one-to-one semi-structured interviews in small focus groups. These were then piloted by the participants as part of the workshop. The focus groups allowed time for participants to build rapport with each other before conducting the one-to-one interviews. The researchers conclude that this short-term approach enabled both the knowledge produced and the processes of participation to be included. Communicative rationality and communal autonomy were addressed by providing opportunities for participants to be involved in learning about, designing and conducting research. Action rationality and individual autonomy were addressed by enabling participants to recommend topics for use in interviews about decision-making for prostate cancer treatment. They point out that participants preferred to have known what the next step in the research was going to be, and as this workshop had been conducted as part of a work in progress this information was not available. Incorporating short-term participation as part of a planned research programme would be of value.

Researcher as instrument of interpretation

Interpretation of data aims to find meaning. In statistically based research this may be achieved by selecting appropriate tests to bring to the data. In qualitative research it may be about bringing theories that aim to get to 'the truth of the matter' (Willig, 2012, p. 11), usually in a theory-driven way to access what lies behind the face value of words or other expressions of experience. This is known as **suspicious interpretation** because it explores the data by reading it through selected lenses to uncover latent meanings. By contrast, **empathic interpretation** seeks to 'elaborate and amplify the meaning that is contained within the material that presents itself' (Willig, 2012, p. 13). The interpreter selects particular features of the data to pay particular attention to in their quest to increase understanding of it. Although the role of the researcher as instrument seems most obvious in this latter form of interpretative process, whenever a researcher analyses data it is through the questions they ask of and about the material that means that they are interpreting it.

RESEARCH EXAMPLE

Summary of research from A. Peshkin (2000). The nature of interpretation in qualitative research. *Educational Researcher, 29*, 5–9.

In a study of the academic achievements of Native American youth Peshkin (2000) sought to illuminate the relationship of researcher subjectivity to the decision points of the interpretation process. By highlighting counterpoints that he labelled 'problematics' this researcher showed where alternative interpretive decisions could have been made in his study. He points out that interpretation is present from the beginning of the research process, using the example of labelling the phenomenon of the study as 'dual-world identity' which immediately points to particular bodies of literature.

It is easy to see that this can be the case in a range of studies of human populations, from medical patients who can be regarded as 'cases' or 'consumers' (e.g. Oakley, 1984) to young mothers who can be regarded as 'opportunistic' or 'making more of their lives' (Phoenix, 1991). Peshkin's interpretive journey ranges from gaining access to participants (thus shaping boundaries, emphases and directions) through assumptions about participants' observed behaviour (as unmotivated and non-persisting) arising from the researcher's personal understandings and reasonings to questioning whether findings made from the research were supporting prior interests brought to it by the researcher. It demonstrates not only the role of the researcher as an instrument who brings subjectivity to the research but also that the interpretation process is present from the beginning of the research. The questions, images and ideas that shape the starting point of the study inform where the researcher chooses to look, their judgement as to what documentation they choose to collect for its substantiation and the ongoing focus of inquiry. The interpretation process throughout is:

> a perspectival accounting for what I have learned, or the shaping of the meanings and understandings of what has gone on from some point of view (Peshkin, 2000, p. 9).

Peshkin's study is also useful in understanding how suspicious and empathic interpretation can be related. Suspicious interpretation uses clues in the data to find out what 'really happened' (Willig, 2012). It does not take the material at face value and instead seeks out latent meanings in it that may be obscured or not immediately obvious. To do this it uses theoretical formulations, a famous example of which is psychoanalysis in which the notion of the unconscious and the significance of childhood relationships is brought to the examination and explanation of adult behaviour. Testing the validity of theories is not the aim of suspicious interpretation. Instead it aims to provide explanations of the manifestation of the data by generating accounts that can explain its manifestation. Suspicious interpretation explains why things are presented as they are and seeks to go beneath the surface to identify and explore underlying processes and structures.

Empathic interpretation stays with the material that presents itself and seeks to elaborate and amplify its meaning (Willig, 2012). Interpretation is not of what lies beneath but of what is manifest. It attends to the features and qualities of the material, looking for connections between them and patterns amongst them. The interpreter has to try and understand from within the phenomenon being described, rather than bringing outside ideas and concepts to it. Interpreters may explore how a person talks about an issue, when the issue is provoked for them and the physiological and affective changes associated with it. Empathic interpretation seeks not only to understand a phenomenon from another's point of view but to also understand its meaning to the person experiencing it.

The two approaches to interpretation are not in opposition. Ricoeur (1996) points out that neither explanation (suspicious interpretation) nor understanding (empathic interpretation) are sufficient on their own to generate satisfactory insight into a phenomenon. Neither 'a reduction of understanding to empathy' nor 'a reduction of explanation to an abstract combinatory system' (see Willig, 2012, p. 15) provide a 'dialectic of understanding and explanation' (Ricoeur, 1996, pp. 153–154 in Willig, 2012). The researcher as instrument of interpretation can seek to combine these philosophical approaches by striving to be close enough to the research to find meaning within it yet far enough from it to evaluate it with reflexivity and theory.

Chapter summary

This chapter has discussed what a researcher does when they carry out the tasks of the research process and has highlighted the subjective role played by them in this. It has considered the objective researcher as an instrument that decides on what tests and measures to bring to data and the subjective researcher as the instrument of the research. The objective researcher brings subjectivity to the role by their agency over the choice of tests. Whilst decisions are largely informed by the research design and the hypothesis under test, extra factors such as a quest for control in the experiment can be introduced by the researcher. A research example illustrated that this can often be as much to be seen to be taking steps towards control as for introducing control itself. Overtly subjective researchers such as those using qualitative research approaches face different challenges arising from being the research instrument itself. Questions are raised about how these 'instruments' can be regarded as credible in the absence of evaluation criteria. Examples showed that personal characteristics can influence how researchers as instruments operate and that this can be particularly challenging when they are trying to develop rapport and conversational space with participants or when researching sensitive topics. The chapter discussed the role of emotional labour in research and how this can be useful to researchers considering the effects of personal emotions and feelings on research. Risk and silence in research were discussed in relation to how researchers can manage, negotiate and understand these, to the benefit of the research and its participants as well as to themselves. All of these areas of the researcher as instrument can be prepared for and anticipated by preparation and planning at the outset of the research, which can include considering not only the effect personally of the research but also ways in which as research instruments researchers can consider how they perform and construct each task in ways that are less likely to bring unwanted subjective bias. The recognition that the instrument role can change as the research progresses can equip researchers to consider in more depth not only what they are doing in research but also how they are doing it and how this is influenced by personal factors. The chapter ended by considering two models of conducting research that recognise and enable the researcher as instrument to take their place within it.

Hints and tips

■ Considering what role you are going to play in the research from the outset can enable clearer thinking about whether and how you are going to be the instrument of the research.

■ Incorporating the notion that the research you conduct will necessarily involve you to greater or lesser degrees and at different points in the research process will provoke careful thinking about the influence you may have on it.

■ Objective researchers can remain detached in the research conduct but also have subjective agency over the choice of tests and measures and the ways that questions are constructed.

■ Subjective researchers recognise their role as instruments of the research and can carry out this role to a high standard by preparing for it. Preparations may include careful thinking about how to elicit data in ways that promote security and trust for participants, anticipation of ways in which they may be affected by the research and planning for negotiating unexpected personal effects.

■ Being clear about what models and measures are being brought to the research and why these have been selected will enhance the credibility of the researcher as instrument.

■ Using support resources to discuss concerns can also highlight unnoticed effects and help the researcher to understand the impact the research has had on them.

■ Recognising changes in the way the research is being carried out can empower the researcher as instrument to investigate the role they have played in bringing about or colluding with these changes.

Further reading

Broom, A., Hand, K., & Tovey, P. (2009). The role of gender, environment and individual biography in shaping qualitative interview data. *International Journal of Social Research Methodology*, *12*(1), 51–65.

Carroll, K. (2012). Infertile? The emotional labour of sensitive and feminist research methodologies. *Qualitative Research*, *13*(5), pp. 546–561.

Fink, A. S. (2000). The role of the researcher in the qualitative research process: A potential barrier to archiving qualitative data. *Forum: Qualitative Social Research*, *1*(13), Art. 4.

Gemignani, M. (2011). Between researcher and researched: An introduction to countertransference in qualitative inquiry. *Qualitative Inquiry*, *17*(8), 701–708.

Lueptow, L. B., Moser, S. L., and Pendleton, B. (1990). Gender and response effects in telephone interviews about gender characteristics. *Sex Roles*, 22(1/2), 29–41.

Roulston, K. (2010). *Reflective interviewing: A guide to theory and practice.* Thousand Oaks, CA: Sage Publications.

Willig, C. (2012). *Qualitative interpretation and analysis in psychology.* New York: McGraw Hill.

Team-based research

4

Chapter map and outcomes

This chapter considers the researcher working as part of a team. It discusses key issues of working as a team member and the practical, theoretical and empirical benefits this offers to individuals and to the research. The chapter begins by defining different ways in which teams of researchers are constructed. It then considers how researchers working within one paradigm and researchers working across paradigms can work with differences to create effective research dialogue. The chapter considers teams made up of researchers from different disciplines and teams of researchers from academic and practice-based settings. It looks at ways in which being one of a team of researchers can enhance the quality of research by drawing attention to the role, decision-making, queries and employment of methods and it describes various methods by which team-based research has been shown to be most effective. The chapter ends with tips and strategies for improving successful team-based research.

Having read this chapter, readers will:

- Understand different ways in which research teams can be constructed
- Have identified some of the key roles of research team members
- Recognise the challenges and the benefits of conducting research as part of a team
- Have considered ways of recognising and negotiating challenges and enhancing benefits
- Be equipped with practical tips and support for working effectively as a member of a research team.

Introduction

> **Researcher View**
>
> 'I think that from my perspective it's interesting and actually I do quite enjoy learning about how other people approach things and how they deal with them and what's important to them.'

Team-based research allows perspectives from different professional, academic and cultural settings and different disciplines and people to be brought together in the study of one topic. If the teamwork is appropriately managed, the benefits of bringing a range of personal experiences to the work can also help to identify new issues and clarify confusions and misunderstandings. Practically, the distribution of and collaboration on common tasks such as literature searching and ethics applications can reduce workload and speed up the time taken for the research to be conducted. Working as a team can provide fertile ground for supervision, discussion and querying of the research as it progresses. There can be challenges, too. These may be differences between team members about how knowledge is constituted, different interests in the research topic or different agendas for conducting the research in the first place. Differences in skill, knowledge and use of methods can lead to biases by some team members toward one research approach over another. Differences between academic researchers and practitioner researchers working together on a team can lead to different priorities in the conduct of the research. As with group work in any domain, team-based research can be dominated by one person or subset of people or can lead to indecision and lack of agreement that may inhibit the progress of the work.

However, effective communication that enables dialogue amongst team members can address some of these challenges. Identified differences in research focus can lead to the development of novel and complex research questions to address a previously unresearched aspect of a topic; combining methods from different domains can illuminate findings in data not possible by the use of one method alone; and different personal perspectives on political, cultural and societal issues can enable transformative insight into key issues. Some researchers (e.g. Katsiaficas, Futch, Fine & Sirin, 2011) use the dialogue between researchers as an additional tool to develop, analyse and interpret data. Before considering some of these issues in detail, however, it is useful to first consider the different ways in which teams are structured and defined.

What is a 'team of researchers'?

Researcher View

'Is that enjoyable [researching as part of a team]? I don't know if that's enjoyable or if that is more satisfactory, kind of useful. I'm trying to think, what's the enjoyable bit? I suppose the enjoyable bit is actually when you do work well as a team and you reach, you know, things in the research that you wouldn't otherwise because it's through the collaboration and complementary expertise that you get to a point that perhaps you wouldn't have otherwise in the end.'

Team-based research is widespread and frequently encouraged by universities and other research institutions but it is understood in different ways. Apart from the hierarchies that develop within many teams (for more on this see later in this chapter), there are a number of operational definitions. Some of these are:

- Multidisciplinary teams: consisting of members who work alongside each other to each bring their specific disciplinary perspective to a commonly agreed research problem.
- Interdisciplinary teams: consisting of members who work together to address an agreed research problem, often selecting a dominant approach or agreeing a mixture of approaches.
- Transdisciplinary teams: consisting of members bringing together discipline-specific theories, concepts and approaches to develop and use a shared conceptual framework to address a common problem (from Slatin, Galizzi, Devereaux Melillo & Mawn, 2004).

One of the first tasks in any research is to agree the research focus and the questions that will be asked by the study. Simple as this sounds it can be a particularly challenging process when working with others, particularly if team members come from different disciplinary backgrounds, have different research approaches, agendas and priorities and unequal amounts of time available for the research. Differences in research questions arise in part from disciplinary backgrounds and foci but also from researcher biographies, interests and priorities.

Effective team-based research seeks out the highest level of expertise by inviting individuals to the team who are knowledgeable in different spheres and methods relevant to the topic under investigation. This may mean inviting practitioners in the field and representatives from the group forming the focus of the investigation to work with academic researchers, for example. Team-based academic research may choose to employ only one method and to actively incorporate a different employment of the method or to gather a team of experts in different methods to focus on one data corpus.

Team members can expect a clear rationale for their inclusion in the team and in turn to be accountable for providing a clear rationale for their contribution to the team. In academic research this may mean being explicit about their employment of a method, a willingness to maintain field journals to consider and clarify their rationale and being open to discussion and querying of their choice and employment of a method. In research conducted between researchers, the researched and practitioners, there is a requirement for a common language to be established to ensure full comprehension of the process and decisions being made in the research process and a willingness to learn more of the perspectives of all those involved.

Researcher View

'I think it shows the importance of knowing each other in working with clinicians or at least kind of having some sort of insight into how the world works for them. Well they do have different priorities and they are working under different management regimes. Whilst we were working on this, there was also an initiative from the hospital management over the development of another initiative that they wanted to put into place whilst this project was ongoing that could have competed with what we were trying to do and it could have gone against, kind of, what we had gathered. So they themselves, the nurses who we were working with on the project, they themselves were also having to come and negotiate with management to say can you just hold off on this for a bit whilst you do this.'

Reflective Question: What skills could you bring to a team of researchers? These may derive from your research knowledge experience, particular expertise in research methods that you have or specialist practice knowledge.

Individual team members have a responsibility to be clear about what they can contribute to the team, just as the team as a whole has a responsibility to be clear about what is expected of each of its members. Realistic appraisal of the skills and expertise of each member, along with identification of the time that each member can offer to the team, will enable more efficient teamworking. Without this, the team risks a lack of cohesion that can adversely influence not only the progress of the research but also its quality. Team members may feel unclear about issues of team leadership and administration or feel that their contributions to the research are insufficiently recognised in its development and outcomes. This can lead to the disintegration of teams or the development of the research in unplanned directions. Similarly, some team members may have greater roles to play at different phases of the research process than at others. The data-gatherer role, for example, may require more engagement during the data collection, analysis and writing-up phases than during the dissemination and implementation into practice phases of the research process.

Some key roles and tasks in research teams

Team Leader/ Project Director	Responsible for recruiting team members, planning the research project timetable, clarifying and assigning tasks to each member, supervising the carrying out of the tasks, overseeing the development of the research project as a whole, developing mechanisms for regular review, organising team meetings and report writing, and working with team members to anticipate and manage conflicts and areas of difference in the research and between team members.
Administrator	Responsible for ensuring documents for ethical approval are prepared and submitted to appropriate bodies, collating associated documents such as Informed Consent sheets as the research progresses, organising dissemination and other events associated with the research, administering expenses claims from participants and researchers, and overseeing and managing the project budget.
Documenter	Keeping records of the progress of the research, both for the team and for the research funders. These may be logs and minutes of meetings, reports and reviews of the research and summaries of the research outcomes.

Expert Participant	Ensures end users have greater presence and power in the research process. This may be by inclusion in the grant-holding team, in 'trial steering groups' and/or advisory/user groups (Tarpey, 201). The design of studies with short-term participation activities is a valuable way of broadening the range of participants (Branney Strickland, Darby, White & Jain, 2016).
Participant Recruiter	Responsible for locating potential participants and networks and settings from which potential participants may be drawn, identifying and approaching potential participants, ensuring that documentation related to ethical considerations for participant involvement are available and completed, and ensuring that participants have all the information they require before agreeing to participate in the research.
Data Gatherer	Responsible for administering tests, conducting interviews and observations (as relevant to the research project) and ensuring that the data is recorded in appropriate ways for analysis and stored confidentially in secure locations.
Data Analyst	Responsible for developing and applying agreed coding systems, carrying out agreed analysis or testing of data, and the recording and reporting of the analysis in ways accessible to the other members of the team.
Report Writer	Responsible for developing agreed reviews and progress reports as the research progresses and writing up the research study and outcomes for wider dissemination.

It is important to note that more than one team member may be involved in all or some of the tasks and that task assignment may vary with the life of the project.

Reflective Question: Which of the tasks listed above would appeal to you as a research team member? Think about the time you might have available to contribute to the team and your personal characteristics and skills that make you more suited to some tasks than others.

It is through the identification and assignment of these tasks that some of the challenges to effective teamworking can be successfully negotiated. Cultivating an openness to communication amongst team members can help with this by encouraging volunteering, questioning and diversity in how the tasks are assigned and carried out. Open communication can foster a commitment to the team as well as to finding ways to work across interpersonal and professional differences that can arise in team-based working. Professional differences in how research is regarded can exist in teams made up of practitioner researchers and academic researchers – the former usually including research amongst many other practice-based tasks, the latter usually regarding research as a key and central role in their academic career. Differences in professional status can determine how much time different team members have available to contribute to the research project. Similarities in professional status or pre-existing connections can shape the effectiveness of communication between team members.

Other differences that can arise in team-based research are founded on the disciplinary and methodological perspectives of team members. This can be the key asset to a team but also an area that can engender and threaten team members' sense of identity and value:

Researcher View

'I think one of the key things that I've learned is that it's about the clarity, so clarity of roles and understanding objectives, who's responsible for what. I think the other thing is openness, so to go into it with an open mind, people in different roles think about things differently to the role that you do. But I think also to retain your identity. So if you're in a team that is an interdisciplinary team and usually that's the reason why you would have a team I think, in my area at least, you know you are there as... so then I'm there as a health psychologist so an important goal for me is to make sure that I actually do things the way that I think a health psychologist should, you know, I don't get persuaded into doing things in a different way. So, yeah, there's that, so clarity, I think openness and maintaining your sense of identity I guess as a professional.'

In the research example below Slatin et al. (2004) study the promotion of healthy and safe employment in healthcare by conducting research with a multidisciplinary team. Their work illustrates the differences and similarities in how team members from the disciplines of community psychology, epidemiology, political science and economics approached the topic.

RESEARCH EXAMPLE

Summary of research from C. Slatin et al., (2004). Conducting interdisciplinary research to promote healthy and safe employment in health care: Promises and pitfalls. *Public Health Reports, 119*, 60–72.

Researchers who had worked together to form the research proposal for a funded study of 'Health Disparities among Health Care Workers' agreed to study whether the socio-economic gradient in health can be explained by different working conditions. They sought to understand differences in how health and health status is understood by different disciplines so that they could address potential conflicts in conducting the research from the outset. They organised a retreat in which four members of the team, an epidemiologist, an economist, a political scientist and a community psychologist, described how their disciplines would approach the research topic. The team discussed the different conceptualisations and found key differences between how each discipline regarded health and health status.

The epidemiologist sought to identify causal mechanisms provoked by features of the participants' jobs and workplaces, to understand how the relationships between socio-economic status and health status are shaped.

The economist sought to focus on issues of relative wages, job status and fairness in promotion practices amongst the participants, to develop more precise estimates of the socio-economic/health status relationships.

The political scientist sought to examine who has control over economic distribution and so has the power to determine health outcomes, in order to explain the relationship.

The community psychologist sought to focus on participants' families, co-workers, hospitals, the healthcare system and societal values about work and income distribution, to study interactions between individuals and environmental influences and their variations over time so that the ways in which participants make sense of externally observable events can be considered in relation to their socio-economic and health status.

The study shows that different goals, and strategies to address them, can arise from different foci and questions of different disciplines. By sharing these perspectives in effective dialogue, these researchers were able to understand the limits of each and work to develop a new and more holistic understanding of the phenomenon.

This study emphasises the value of open dialogue amongst researchers working as a team. It allowed for different ways of regarding and querying a topic and for these to be made transparent. In turn, this enabled new approaches for exploring it to be developed. These researchers achieved this through organised retreats and also the provision of seminars that educated each member about the others' disciplines and their approaches.

Organised meetings and workshops for teams of researchers can provide a useful way of encouraging the sharing of knowledge and research methodology. This does not take away from the responsibility for each researcher to consider their individual stance on the research throughout the research process. A key way of doing this is through a reflexive approach that sets up a dialogue between researchers about the research they are undertaking. Working this way can be conducive to interpersonal relationships as well as to the quality of the ensuing research and its outcomes. In the next section, ways in which reflexivity can be practised in team-based research are discussed.

Practising reflexivity in research teams

Reflexivity requires a researcher to consider what they bring to the research and how this impacts on the research process. It explicitly includes consideration of the researcher and how they are conducting the research, by making more transparent the relationship between the researcher and the research itself. Earlier chapters have discussed that for individual researchers this can mean an enhanced awareness of their positionality, and changes in their positionality, during the conduct of the research. In turn, this enables them to be better able to understand the data they have gathered and their interpretation of it (see Chapter 2 for more on researcher positionality). This awareness is beneficial to the rigour and quality of the research. In qualitative research, reflexivity is regarded as a quality criterion. In quantitative research, where researchers are expected to remain objective in relation to the research they are conducting, the role of researcher autobiography has led to the questioning of objectivity when assessing the extent to which research is a rigorous test of theory or hypothesis (Carter & Hurtado, 2007). By considering their personal interests in the research topic, distinctions between a researcher's own observations and the views of the same phenomenon by others can be made. In quantitative research this has important implications for reliability and validity of the research.

Conducting research as a researcher who is part of a team raises further issues about reflexivity. No longer is the relationship between the researcher and the research the only consideration. Additionally, each researcher must also consider their relationships with other researchers and how these relationships shape and inform the research process. The relationships with other researchers may of course be interpersonal but they will also include dialogues about different theories, methods and approaches to the research.

Personal reflection about the relationships with others in the team can aid the development of a team-wide reflexive dialogue being set up. Both individual and group subjectivities and the relationships between them can be better considered and researchers better enabled to make transitions between and amongst the relationships, dynamics and dialogues that evolve and emerge throughout the research process. If this approach to group reflexivity is successful, a valuable plurality of all the voices of the research process is generated and expanded understandings of the research can be achieved (Russell & Kelly, 2002). Better research strategies can be generated through openness to the knowledge of others in the team.

In addition, an awareness of the personal attributes and approaches of team members to their work can bring a useful sensitivity when the research approach differs or develops in a different direction to a team member's usual method.

RESEARCH EXAMPLE

Summary of research from G. M. Russell & N. H. Kelly (2002). Research as interacting dialogic processes: Implications for reflexivity. *Forum: Qualitative Social Research*, *3*(3), Art 18.

Russell and Kelly provide the example of a team member who appeared to hear respondents' accounts as 'sad' more often than other members of the team did. Reflective group discussions allowed insight into personal events which revealed the team member had recently ended a personal relationship. Team discussion highlighted that this may have made him more sensitive than the other researchers to hearing sadness in respondents' data and that he might identify it in places in the data that the other team members did not. The team context of the research meant that other team members were also enabled to become more sensitised to this dimension of the data, as individuals and as a team. It became possible for all to see the data from perspectives that they may not otherwise have been able to and to see more than they may otherwise have done.

Reflexivity as a team also allows for questions to emerge as a consequence of being asked for clarification by 'outsider' members – those who do not share the same knowledge or discipline base as 'insider' members of the team. By having to address questions that they consider they already know the answer to, team members have to consider their knowledge again and be prepared to acknowledge assumptions and biases that they may inherently hold and be imposing on to the interpretation of participants' data. Thus, when bringing reflexivity to team research, contradictions and gaps in research findings are more likely to be identified and explored rather than obscured or cast aside.

Reflective Question: Imagine you have conducted research into the effects of mental illness on parenting. You found a significant theme described by the participants in your study was that of the difficulties in being heard as a parent by professionals involved in mental healthcare provision. You are invited on to a research team that wishes to develop an intervention for parents seeking support for parenting in large families. How would you explain the relevance of mental illness in parenting to fellow team members, who comprise a psychologist, a social worker and a social policy researcher?

Team-based reflexivity is not without its challenges. On a personal level, researchers may feel reluctant or embarrassed to reveal personal biographies that inform their research interest (e.g. Frost et al., 2012). They may be concerned that they appear less competent than fellow researchers or frustrated at the perceived lower level of knowledge of other researchers. When decisions are made about how to report research findings from a team, individuals may feel overexposed or undervalued if only one paradigm or clear finding is presented as the coherent outcome of the research.

The following research example below highlights ways in which individual and team reflexivity become salient, and are enacted, with variations in team structure and associated dynamics.

RESEARCH EXAMPLE

Summary of research from C. A. Barry, N. Britten, N. Barber, C. Bradley, & F. Stevenson (1999). Using reflexivity to optimise teamwork in qualitative research. *Qualitative Health Research, 9*(1), 26–44.

The study: The project studied doctor–patient communication about prescribing in general practice. Its aim in Phase 1 was to fully explore the paradox of doctors complaining about patients 'demanding' prescriptions and patients complaining that doctors overprescribe. The aim of Phase 2 was to use the information gained in Phase 1 to design and evaluate educational interventions.

Phase 1 comprised 62 case studies of patients in 20 practices. Patients were interviewed using semi-structured interviews. Doctors audiotaped consultations with patients and were subsequently interviewed about their perceptions of the consultations. Patients were interviewed again a week after the consultation about their views and subsequent actions. The interviews were gathered with the aim of linking expectations and perceptions of patients and doctors about a specific consultation to what actually happened in the consultation and what the patients did with their medicines after it.

Research team structure: The team size and make-up changed over the course of the study, initially including three project directors and subsequently recruiting two research fellows. Job changes led to the relocation of one of the project directors when they were promoted to a Chair in Ireland. The project changed to incorporate an additional site in Ireland for the recruitment of doctors and patients. Phase 2 needed only one part-time research fellow researcher and the second research fellow moved to a linked project.

Reflexive evaluation: The changing dynamics of the team meant that the initially comfortable working relationship that the three project directors enjoyed had to be expanded and renegotiated with the addition of the two research fellows. They worried that the new team would not mesh as well and the new members worried whether there would be space for their input. Knowing that the team would have to be reduced for Phase 2 of the study brought additional anxieties.

Prior to the team expansion from three to five members, the three project directors had equal responsibilities for the development of the project and its shared goals. The three members were of equal status and age. With the addition of the two researchers, the dynamics changed so that there was reluctance from team members to take the lead on issues or to formalise roles. This compromised efficiency and introduced a greater hierarchy into the team, arising from the split in the workload. Only the researchers were responsible for participant recruitment and fieldwork, meaning that they had different agendas and goals to those of the project directors. This created a two-tier team structure.

When the data had been collected, the researchers were responsible for conducting all the analysis for the early writing. The project directors became consultants, editors, project overseers and the liaison points with the funders.

Overall, efficiency, feelings and communication varied at each point of the changing team structure.

This team of authors/researchers identified a number of other challenges to the effectiveness of the team.

(i)   Place and time: being located across four sites reduced the opportunities for informal and face-to-face meetings. This meant that it took longer for the group to bond socially and there were fewer possibilities for developing new ideas with each other. There were also technological issues requiring agreement of standardised documentation sent by email that was compatible with the software of all members of the team. As team members were located within different universities, this meant negotiating three different electronic systems. Changes in employment or upgrades to systems required renegotiation.

(ii) Data analysis: to increase the rigour of the research the whole team was involved in the data analysis. Requirements of each member's role within the university meant that the project directors did not have sufficient time for equal involvement. To counter this, the project directors developed the coding framework and the researchers took over the subsequent analysis of the data. In this way, the team was able to capitalise on the multidisciplinary insight of the team to increase the conceptual development. Organised discussions amongst the team enabled training for the analysts to look for issues in the data that they would not otherwise have considered. A series of subsequent negotiations enabled different coding schemes to be developed: one for each case study and one for cross-case analysis. Data was split and delegated to a researcher for analysis.

(iii) Writing responsibilities: to avoid conflict about authorship of papers to be published from the research, a policy was agreed upon by the three project directors before recruitment of the researchers.

The study shows that the team membership, changes in it and the accompanying dynamics are relevant to all stages of the research. From the study's outset contracts about roles and responsibilities can go a long way to anticipating and addressing difficulties that can arise in areas of leadership, writing, communication expectations and the various tasks of research practice. This team managed these challenges to some extent by recognising the value of communication and by seeking an openness to feelings of anxiety and defensiveness amongst team members. With this they were able to cohere around different perspectives, availabilities and involvement in the research project, with an eye to its rigour and successful completion.

In the words of another researcher who has worked on research teams:

Researcher View

'I think it's better than working on your own. So although there are challenges they make it exciting and, you know, a lot, so much about working in an applied field like I do is about building up relationships and building networks and stuff and so that is a really important part of research that sometimes is kind of under-sung, you know we can be an amazing analyst, but if we can't get on with people then that's going to be a problem. So yes it's much better I would say. There are pros and cons I suppose, working on your own is good if you kind of, you know, really need to draw down into something, but I think there's more benefit perhaps to working with other people.'

With attention paid to pragmatic aspects of team-based research, concerns about rigour and credibility of the outcomes of the research can start to be addressed. Central to these is the negotiation and incorporation of the choice and use of different methods and methodologies that different team members bring to the team.

Team-based research and methodology

Methodology is frequently discussed as though each paradigm has a static meaning and is applied universally. Discussions in this book so far have shown the relevance of subjectivity within different paradigms and how subjectivity can fluctuate within and across research conducted by different researchers depending on their positionality, research priorities and motivation for doing the research. The range of methods within qualitative and quantitative approaches allows different methods to be employed within each paradigm and for the same methods to be used differently by different researchers. Team structure most usually seeks out expertise in different research methods in order to construct teams that bring multiple perspectives and insight into a research problem but there can also be value in each team member applying the same method. This can highlight differences not only in application of method but also in adherence to and perception of underlying tenets of the method. The outcome can illuminate different meanings in data, on a spectrum ranging from convergence in meanings to contradiction between them.

A study conducted by King et al. (2008) aimed to explore the use of one method by different researchers making up a team in a study of the 'psychology of mistrust'. Each member of the team was an expert in using interpretative phenomenological analysis (IPA), 'an approach to qualitative, experiential and psychological research which has been informed by concepts and debates from three key areas of philosophy of knowledge: phenomenology, hermeneutics and idiography' (Smith, Flowers, & Larkin, 2009, p. 11). IPA draws on each of these theoretical approaches to inform its distinctive epistemological framework and research methodology and to explore phenomena of lived experience by individuals. (For more on the use and applications of IPA see Shinebourne (2011) in Frost (2011).) The study and its key findings are described and discussed in the box below:

RESEARCH EXAMPLE

Summary of research from N. King et al. (2008). 'Can't really trust that, so what can I trust?': A polyvocal, qualitative analysis of the psychology of mistrust. *Qualitative Research in Psychology*, 5(2), 80–102.

The study: An exploration of the 'psychology of mistrust' was carried out by five researchers who separately analysed the transcript of a semi-structured interview conducted by a sixth team member to elicit data from a participant about her experience of mistrust. Each researcher analysed the transcript using a phenomenological method and with the aim of being descriptive rather than explanatory. The team then discussed the individual analyses as a group to reach a consensual analysis and individual analyses. On reaching the consensual analysis each team member was asked to adjust their individual descriptive analysis to represent their readings of the data that had been excluded from the group reading. The individual analyses were then written up by another member of the team to highlight different emphases brought to the analysis by individual analysts.

The findings:
Themes identified in the consensual analysis:

> Associated undermining of self/identity
> Embodied emotional turmoil
> Pervasive spread of unease
> An attempt to recover self-identity
> An attempt to recover social grounding

Themes identified in individual analyses:

> Metaphor and symbol
> The interview as occasioned interaction
> The rhetorical structure of the mistrust narrative
> Embodied subjectivity: reflections on the interview process

Discussion: The evaluation of the group research process for these researchers created a tension. On the one hand, the analysts agreed that the disjuncture between the consensual analysis and the individual analyses highlighted powerful findings and valuable reflexivity that enabled them to attend to both the contextual and the experiential dimensions of the research process. The consensual analyses allowed a rich but incomplete insight into the world of the participant and one that could not have been achieved by bringing only one researcher to the process. On the other hand, the differences amongst the individual commentaries led the group to question the status of the differences. They queried the presentation of the different epistemological positions, the coherence of the research aims and methods reflected and whether the different accounts provide different facets of experience that may be complementary to, even if incompatible with, each other. The interviewer argued that a positive evaluation of the researcher experience enabled differences between the researcher and the researched to be reduced and minimised individual unelucidated prejudices dominating the research.

This team of researchers encountered differences in their applications of a method underpinned by similar ontology and epistemology, which led to some meanings being found that did not fit with the consensus. The differences led to difficulties in producing an integrated account of the meanings within the data. Group discussions focused on how to consider them in relation to the consensus and in relation to how each researcher had employed the method of analysis. In this study, the researchers concluded that the degree of commonality and consensus of meanings within the data meant that this was what should be privileged rather than differences in reflexivity amongst the researchers.

The interviewer, however, strikes another note and suggests that without considering and evaluating the researcher role, the hierarchy between researcher and researched can mean that it is the researcher view that comes to, perhaps unknowingly, dominate the research interpretation. This presents a challenging problem for research teams, as they must battle through identification of differences in uses of methods and also in personal world views. This can risk introducing threat and vulnerability to individual members of the research team and a questioning of the value of working with difference. With the aim of working together to rigorously analyse data to produce an integrated, agreed upon and useful account, researchers also have to consider individual differences in their research conduct and how these are integrated into the team.

Other research, such as that of Frost et al. (2010), in which different methods were brought by each team member to the analysis of the same data, has shown that attention to the role of individual reflexivity of researchers working in the team can allow further insight into how new research questions can emerge from the research and help to identify appropriate additional methods to bring to it. As in the example above, each member of the team has to account for their choice and use of method to the other team members in consideration of the research focus and describe the limitations and constraints of the different methods in exploring the data. By discussing their experience of the analysis with each other, researchers come to recognise aspects of the subjective and reflexive use of their method, sometimes within distinct epistemological contexts. In the study by Frost et al. (2010) this enabled researchers to identify that they had each developed a character for the narrator and a picture of her social world based only on their reading of the interview transcript. Each researcher also expressed emotion toward the narrator – ranging from affection to sympathy to frustration about her perception of herself as a mother. This presented difficulties for the researchers in how to present the narrator as she changed positions and meanings throughout her account. The group discussions enabled these and other tensions in the individual roles of the analysts to be highlighted and shared, leading to review and changes of the research findings including the inclusion of some that had been initially discarded. This development and use of group reflexivity enabled the researchers to focus on their roles in the research process rather than simply on the role of the method. This reduces the risk of methodolatry (Curt, 1984), in which the research method becomes more important than the research focus, creeping into research practice.

> **Reflective Question:** What is your preferred method of data collection and analysis? Think about why this is. What was the role of your research training in determining your knowledge of this method and in limiting your knowledge of other methods?

Team-based research and objectivity

Reflexivity does not play as explicit a role in quantitative research as it does in qualitative research but some researchers have called for its consideration in the conduct of rigorous quantitative research. Quantitative research regards participants and researchers as acting independently of each other in the research process. 'Gold standard' designs such as double-blind placebos are used to control bias and subjectivity of both and little or no attention is paid to the participants or the data collector in correlational studies. However, many researchers insist that the intersection of researcher autobiography with quantitative research practice is just as important to consider as it is in qualitative research practice (e.g. Carter & Hurtado, 2007). Team-based quantitative research may enable this intersection and its role in the research to be made more explicit.

Carter and Hurtado (2007) point out that research is often carried out by researchers because of personal experiences and a sense of being under-represented. Such researchers may seek to test intuitive hypotheses about how the world works, formed from an understanding that there is something unique about their experience and the overcoming of the odds of failure that deserves explanation. They state that recognising this:

> ...drives us to develop better questions, more relevant models for diverse student populations, and to understand whether the issues of this generation of students are the same as for our own generation. With every test of a model using a distinct population, we attempt to break down the theory, document alternative experiences, and begin to construct new models... (Carter & Hurtado, 2007).

Others (e.g. Rothman, Lipset, & Nevitte, 2003) have highlighted that potential political motivation and biases of researchers mean that the autobiography of researchers should be considered when judging not only the rigor of the research but also how it fits into the overall work of researchers in their long-term research goals. Such goals may be to improve or change national policies or services for example.

Objective researchers who conduct team-based research are sometimes carrying out mixed-methods research. They may work alongside both objective and subjective researchers, for example to gather and analyse qualitative data which determines the key focus of subsequent large-scale generalisable research. Mixed-methods research might also be conducted by following a quantitative phase with a qualitative phase in order to enrich the statistical data and add some meanings and depth to the results. In either case the different perspectives that the researchers bring through their methods can be incorporated into the research in what Flick (2011) calls **investigator triangulation**. Investigator triangulation systematically triangulates the different conceptual perspectives brought by the different researchers to develop a **theory triangulation**.

In turn this drives forward a **methodological triangulation**. The outcome of this **comprehensive triangulation** (p. 149) is data access on different levels and with different qualities. Through a mechanism of accountability by researchers, all methods employed are given the same weight and are used systematically. The outcome is a credible integrated reflection of different theoretical backgrounds that have been carefully considered in the methodological planning of the study.

A study conducted by Flick (2010), in which both qualitative and quantitative methods were employed to explore crisis in health and social care, drew on professional, institutional and biographical aspects of the participants in recognition that these concepts influence how social problems are perceived and constructed. The study and evaluation of social problems include a variety of stakeholders, each with varied perspectives on the issue (see also Frost & Nolas, 2013 for more on this).

In applying this approach Flick enables a number of questions to be raised about common understandings and misunderstandings by service providers and service users and the implications of these for researchers.

RESEARCH EXAMPLE

Summary of research from U. Flick (2010). Triangulation of micro-perspectives on juvenile homelessness, health and human rights. In N. K. Denzin & M. D. Giardina (Eds.), *Qualitative inquiry and human rights* (pp. 186–204). Walnut Creek, CA: Left Coast.

The study: Flick's study investigated the health and sickness, the help-seeking behaviour and the institutional perceptions of homeless adolescents in Berlin. Three approaches were employed in the study: observation of the health-focused interactions of the adolescents, episodic interviews with the adolescents about their subjective definitions of health and their living situations, and expert interviews with health and other practitioners working with homeless people.

The findings: The researchers found that adolescents tend to ignore their chronic illnesses, mostly because of general resignation, and that they turn to drugs and alcohol as a coping strategy. Many of the adolescents' accounts referred to negative experiences with physicians and that this prevented them from seeking further help. Interviews showed that professionals found the adolescents' coping strategies to be failing in general and interpreted this as evidence that they were not ready to deal with their disease and its challenges. The observations revealed the problems the adolescents encountered in their communications with professionals.

Flick concludes that the use of different methods brings different levels of insight ranging from social interactionist perspectives on practices and interventions (observation) to internal perspectives from the point of view of the adolescents (interviews) and external perspectives from professionals' points of view (expert interviews). The complementarity of the results also highlights different perspectives of service providers and potential service users and highlights the risk of non-utilisation by service users even in the face of escalating crisis in their lives.

Multiple-researcher mixed-methods research makes unique demands on the time and expertise of researchers. When working alone, researchers have to challenge their competences and preferences in the use of each approach. When working with multiple researchers there is a demand for each to be clear about their choice and employment of epistemological stance, as well as how it has been used in the pursuit of the research question.

By employing multiple researchers, the selection and employment of methods have to be considered in relation to the research question. A rationale for their use has to be constructed. Using multiple researchers allows for the reflexive awareness and engagement with the research process that each researcher brings. Whilst allowing for cross-paradigm, multi-ontological and multi-epistemological readings of data that can bring more salient understandings of the complexities of human experience than mono-method approaches can, multiple-method research demands greater transparency of method, of process and, perhaps most importantly, of researcher, to ensure high-quality work.

Working as a team member within a team that uses both qualitative and quantitative approaches enables ways of making more transparent the impact of each researcher on the process and of clarifying the theoretical foundations of the study to link methods to research questions. Clear statements and sets of actions agreed by all researchers involved have to be present and researchers are expected to provide a rationale for their choice and employment of a method in relation to the research question. Interpretations reached singly can be explained and then discussed as a group.

Reflective Question: If you primarily use quantitative methods in your research and conduct research that seeks to test theories, what would you want to know about research from a researcher who uses qualitative research to seek meanings in data?

Challenges for researchers working in a mixed-methods research team can often arise in finding ways in the research outcomes to include all the methods used. In an extended study by Bryman (2007), several barriers to the integration of qualitative and quantitative approaches were identified. These included limitations imposed by rigid research structures or designs, as one might expect. Another limitation was that of different journals' publication constraints, which were found frequently to emphasise one research approach over another. Of particular interest when considering the researcher role, however, are the findings that researcher skill specialisms influence individuals' approaches to the research and their preference for one method or form of data over another. As a barrier to the integration of mixed methods, this means that some researchers can have an inhibition or incapacity to integrate methods and data. As a consideration of the researcher role when working as part of a team, it is interesting to note that it is not only the methods but the way they are used by researchers that influence good research practice.

The investigation found that the suggestion to develop teams of researchers as one way to overcome the barrier to integration of qualitative and quantitative methods was met with scepticism. Arguments that this would allow both qualitative and quantitative specialists to be brought to the work were countered with a fear that this approach would in fact impede the integration of findings, as researchers would not understand each other's methodological approaches. There was an expectation that specialists from different perspectives would need to be helped to work together in order to find ways for their skills to be welded together. This insight is illustrated well in the following quote from one respondent in the Bryman (2007) study:

> There are sometimes, you know, issues about project management because one is trying to bring together, sometimes in a research team, people with quite different perspectives, and help them to work together on the project and it may not always be very easy if they are very good at the type of research that they do but see themselves as particularly in one camp rather than the other, then you sometimes need to think about ways of helping them to work together (p. 16).

Finding ways of helping researchers work together in mixed-methods teams has led to the development not only of increased awareness of what each approach can bring to the research but also of new research designs in which each researcher is valued for the contribution they bring and each is encouraged to enter into dialogue with the other team members through regular group discussions that aim to help the team to recognise the strengths and constraints of both approaches.

Maintaining a clear focus on the research question also helps to evaluate the employment of different methods. One example of how this can be achieved is in the emergence of qualitatively driven mixed-methods approaches (Hesse-Biber, 2010; Mason, 2006). By regarding methods as tools, Hesse-Biber (2010) points out that a researcher's methodology determines the way in which a tool will be utilised, which in turn can seem problematic for those researchers that know only one methodology and who believe that qualitative and quantitative methodologies are mutually exclusive.

A qualitatively driven approach encompasses several theoretical traditions. All have the common core assumption that social reality is constructed and that subjective meaning is a critical component of knowledge-building. A qualitative tradition recognises the importance of the subjective human creation of meaning but doesn't always reject outright some notion of objectivity (Hesse-Biber, Rodriguez & Frost, 2015). Qualitatively driven mixed-methods approaches privilege qualitatively-driven epistemology and methodology and places quantitative inquiry as secondary in the mixed-methods design. Usually the quantitative component does not stand alone as a separate study and instead is selected for its complementarity to the qualitative component. This approach can be particularly useful in researching topics related to issues of social justice and social change because the qualitative driver of the design explicitly incorporates subjectivity, thus making clear the researcher agenda whilst incorporating descriptions of direct experience from a range of participants.

> **Reflective Question:** How would you turn a research question such as 'What are the working conditions of nurses in intensive-care settings?' into a qualitatively driven mixed-methods research question?

Team-based research and co-operation

Whilst teamworking can provide opportunity for openness and transparency in the development and decision-making of the research process, it is also dependent on co-operation from each of its members. There are numerous stories of research teams seeking to recruit new members with particular skills or knowledge and then marginalising the person and the work they do. This is sometimes because of a tick-box approach to team construction, where teams have obtained funding for their research on the basis that they will include a range of methods but when it comes to conducting the research the work is dominated by a pre-defined agenda. At other times, this is because of the inherent bias towards personal methods of choice, which considers the results of those methods reported over the results of other methods as a barrier to mixing methods, as discussed above (Bryman, 2007).

Practical challenges to co-operation can arise from a lack of understanding by objective researchers of the time needed for qualitative research, resulting in a rushed job for the subjective researchers and a sense of frustration that their work is not being allowed to be fully completed. Similarly, when teams are made up of academic and practitioner researchers there can be a lack of recognition of the role that research plays in the professional lives of different members. Practitioners are often accommodating research into busy practice-based roles, whilst academic researchers may be looking for publications and other research-based activities associated with the conduct of the research in order to further their careers. Academic researchers may be more concerned with epistemological underpinnings of research than practitioners who are keen to see the research progress to a useful conclusion. There may also be a lack of understanding by academic researchers about the professional practices associated with the topic under investigation. Varying agendas and interests in outcomes of research influences can strain relations between academic and practitioner researcher stakeholders who comprise a research team.

Such teams can be made up of members with different research agendas and practices and these can be carried out with different motives and incentives. Researchers in the team may have different cultural, political and geographical locations. With these issues come risks of divisions of knowledge and knowledge production, of decontextualisation, if some researchers are working 'in the field' and others 'in the office' (Mauthner & Doucet, 2008), and of labour, if roles are not clearly identified. Team research works best when each member is clear about what their role in the team is and what the tasks associated with the role are. In practice, tasks range across the group and across the life of the research project. Writing up the research may be a collaborative venture that is led by one of its members or a collective one in which different team members write different sections of the final reports and papers. Contributions to the team may range from intellectual to practical and are often dependent on levels of experience and extant projects and commitments.

One experienced team-based researcher describes the importance of defining and assigning roles as follows:

Researcher View

'I think role is important in terms of what you can contribute in terms of actually what you do as well as availability. So they need to know how much time you're going to allow yourself on this project and how much time the other people on the team can expect you to give to this project. I think clarity of role, also when there are research fellows and research assistants involved in terms of who actually manages them, you know, who is their line manager, do you have more than one person involved in that kind of day-to-day stress, or, you know, affairs? So when we were working on this particular project, the two of us, the social policy person and me, we were working on a qualitative component of a mixed-methods project and so we were both sort of in charge of that and in charge of the research fellow. But because we never really set those roles clearly in the beginning it kind of fell between the both of us and it was quite challenging to actually manage the researcher then, because we didn't quite know who was supposed to be doing what. And then on top of that there was the Principal Investigator who was in charge of everything, so all the different elements to the project and what role did she have. So yes that's why I think role is important.'

To be a researcher within a team, however, can mean that the tasks assigned may not be the ones that are most desired. Agency and control over what happens to the data collected or the other work done by one researcher may be lost in subsequent phases of the research. Acknowledgement of the division of labour may be perceived by other members of the team to be less than it is experienced to be by an individual researcher. Mauthner and Doucet (2008) argue that 'hierarchies of knowledge' (Reay, 2000, p. 19) are created by the higher status accorded to textual knowledge, regarded as more objective, than to the embodied and contextual knowledge generated by the study, regarded as more subjective. These researchers propose that 'While in theory social scientists within a postfoundationalist tradition recognise that knowledge is tied to the contexts, conditions and relations of its production, in practice these are devalued and not drawn upon as sources of knowledge in their own right' (Mauthner & Doucet, 2008, p. 979). They suggest that this arises in part from the political organisation of research, which means that differential status and value of different research tasks and of the researcher carrying them out may mean that the research task or researcher are regarded as having a lower or higher status. A mental/manual division of labour can arise between fieldwork in which data is collected and interpretation and theorisation of the findings (McKenna, 1991, p. 125).

With recognition of the potential within team-based research for researchers to develop effective communication and clear role identification, the practices of team research can be valuable learning experiences. Researchers can learn tasks that range from research conduct to budget management and leadership. The challenge is often to recognise how these experiences can be coherent within a team and to understand their impact on the research itself.

Reflective Question: Of all the tasks and roles necessary for high-quality team-based research to be carried out, which ones would you least like to do? Think about why this is in terms of your skills, interests, expertise and personality. What does this mean for your membership of a research team?

In the next section this chapter turns again to the issue of communication but considers it within the context of virtual teamworking. The heightened importance of sound team management when researchers may never meet each other is discussed and the challenges and benefits of conducting research under these circumstances considered.

Virtual team-based research

Attention to the interpersonal dynamics of team members has been shown to be an important aspect of successful teamworking. It fosters openness and trust and allows for potential conflicts and disagreements to be anticipated and addressed with minimal damage to the research process. Indeed, from a reflexive standpoint the ways in which conflicts are negotiated can lead to a furthering of the research by the identification of new questions or the revisiting of previously agreed foci.

With the development of technology there has been an increase in virtual teamwork. A team made up of researchers based in different geographical locations can utilise virtual communication techniques to work across settings, time zones and cultures and can often bring greater diversity to research projects, along with increased flexibility, motivation and empowerment of team members. With this, though, also comes challenges arising from the decreased likelihood of face-to-face meetings so that members are also at risk of feeling isolated and without support in resolving queries about their role and its challenges as the research develops.

Hertel, Geister and Konradt (2005) define different forms of 'virtual' work as being dependent on the number of people involved and the degree of interaction between them. Whilst the term 'virtual' 'designates distributed work that is predominantly based on electronic information and communication tools' (p. 71) different understandings of virtual teams and groups in management settings can be used to understand different forms of virtual team research.

Summary table of different formations of virtual-based research teams

From G. Hertel, S. Geister & U. Konradt (2005). Managing virtual teams: A review of current empirical research. *Human Resource Management Review,* 15(1), 69–95.

Telework: information and telecommunication services are used to enable a team of researchers to work away from the main research base.

Virtual groups: several researchers work together and each member reports to the same manager.

Virtual teams: members of a virtual group interact with each other in pursuit of common research goals.

Virtual communities: larger groups of researchers, commonly initiated by individual team members rather than central management, in which members communicate via the Internet to achieve common purposes, roles and norms.

Virtual teams have been further defined as:

(i)   Consisting of two or more persons
(ii) Collaborating interactively to achieve common goals
(iii) Having one or more members working at a different location, organisation or time zone
(iv) Communicating predominantly via electronic communication methods (Hertel et al., 2005).

It is important to remember that virtual communication does not have to be the sole interaction of virtual teams. Similarly, it would be incorrect to assume that conventional face-to-face research teams do not use some electronic communication. Thus the *relative* virtuality of a team is a useful way to think about the leadership, challenges and benefits of effective teamwork. Virtuality can be assessed using indicators of the relationship between virtual and face-to-face communication, the number of research sites within one team and the average distance between members. It is probably most common to have a mixture of face-to-face meetings alongside virtual meetings and electronic forms of communication, enabled by email, telephone, Skype and wiki pages. This approach helps to compose a team based on expertise rather than proximity to the research team's leadership base and can utilise insider researcher access to potential participants. Travel and spaces resources can be minimised. However, it also brings challenges to researcher support and supervision, access to training and data security. Perhaps of greatest risk to the research process, however, is the distance within interpersonal relationships as the following example illustrates:

RESEARCH EXAMPLE

Summary of research from N. A. Frost et al. (2012). Pleasure, pain, and procrastination: Reflections on the experience of doing memory-work research, *Qualitative Research in Psychology*, 9(3), 231–248.

Background: The memory-work method was developed by Haug in the late 1970s as a way of flattening hierarchies between researcher and researched and of exploring how women contribute to and are shaped by oppressive practices (Haug 1987). The aim of this study was to explore the process of analysing personal memories triggered by the phrase 'loss of faith'. Each member of the collective of researchers was an expert in particular methods of data analysis, some using the same method but in different ways. Each was based at a different university, some in the UK, and others in different countries in Europe. Research interests ranged from identity to motherhood and emotion but all researchers signed up to working together in a collective exploration of the memory-work method.

Method: At the outset of the study a series of meetings was planned and a wiki page developed to enable electronic discussions. This was in recognition of the geographical distance between researchers and for the same reason a series of Skype meetings was planned in addition to occasional face-to-face meetings to be held in different countries. It is a requirement of the memory-work approach that all analysis is conducted as a group and so these practical steps were important to maximise both the adherence to the guidance of the method and the efficiency with which the research could be conducted.

Findings: Despite this careful planning, it became apparent that trying to find space and time, nationally and virtually, in which all researchers could meet was an insurmountable challenge. Apart from work and family commitments, life events such as pregnancies, illnesses and house moves were features of the collective members' lives. In practice, these events prevented full attendance at all bar two of the meetings held over the course of nearly two years and a Skype meeting with full attendance was never achieved. The development of the wiki page necessitated a degree of individual responsibility for members to add to it and keep abreast of developments documented there – a responsibility that, in practice, was affected by work and varying levels of electronic know-how amongst members.

Implications: Perhaps because of an acceptance of the impossibility of convening together and out of a sense of frustration with the slow advance of the research, a subset of researchers decided at one meeting to analyse the memory of a researcher who was not present. It was only sometime after the event that the incongruity of this approach with the original aim of working as a collective was realised. The memory 'owner' was upset that she had not been present and she disagreed with the outcomes of the analysis of her memory.

She felt that her experience had been obscured in the analysis of her language and that her memory had been 'packed into discursive structures' in her absence. Despite all the aims of memory work and the researchers' desire to work as a collective, the team had ended up with the analysis of a team member's memory that lacked subjectivity.

Conclusion: After some virtual discussion and some more time passing, the memory was re-analysed with the full inclusion of the memory owner but the experience raised questions about the realities of working as a team of researchers. It highlighted how the focus on overcoming practical obstacles and challenges such as those brought about by working at a distance from each other and the consequent meetings of some researchers but not the whole team, obscured the team's attendance to the ethical concerns of working with personal data. The transparent engagement with each other as a collective enabled a revisiting of the process and a new analysis of the data. The use of electronic communication was dependent on each researcher taking responsibility for interacting with it and for all to ensure the inclusion of the whole team in group decisions and actions.

This study highlights how effective teamworking can be hindered by the practicalities of negotiating time and distance amongst a group of people. Even with the specific emphasis on working collectively that the memory-work method requires, this team of researchers were challenged to adhere to full group involvement to the extent that they overlooked this basic tenet of the research practice. To the benefit of the research, the reflexive and open stance that the researchers had striven to bring to the research meant that this serious oversight was recognised and addressed but the distance in geography and interaction seems to have, for a time at least, introduced a distance between the researchers and their research practice.

This risk can be reduced by being open to learning from each team research experience:

Researcher View

'I don't know if there was a plan! [Laughs] Management of those challenges, I think because I was the kind of lead academic on this project and it was I suppose the first one really where I'd had that role. So I was learning on the job and had my eyes opened really. So I wouldn't say I didn't plan at all, but I think next time, I mean I have, I'm just embarking on a new project actually now, not as PI, but as somebody who is kind of in charge of an element of a larger-scale project and I'm now going into this and this is a similar situation. So I know that we have to kind of get clear in advance what people's roles are and who's going to do what and all that sort of thing. So I will be planning for it on this next project, having learned from the experience.'

Chapter summary

This chapter has examined team-based research to consider what is expected of researcher members and how best they can meet these expectations. Key roles and tasks have been identified as well as the importance to the effectiveness of the team of making these clear. Ways in which different structures of teams can influence the perspectives, methods and conduct of research have been discussed in terms of teams of practitioner researchers and academic researchers working together, researchers working across and within methods and paradigms, and teams of researchers made up from different disciplinary backgrounds. The importance and challenges of effective communication strategies to provide support for the generation and development of ideas and for the space for negotiating conflicts have been shown to affect the quality of the research as well as the cohesion of the team. By considering virtual teamworking, particular threats to the quality of the research were identified. Throughout the chapter, questions, research examples and personal insight from team-based researchers have sought to provoke the reader to understand more about researching as part of a team and to consider their own research practice.

Hints and tips

■ Identify the tasks that will be needed to be carried out throughout the research process at the outset of the study.

■ Recognise that the research may require new tasks to be added to the list and that existing tasks may need to be redefined as the research develops.

■ Be prepared for team membership to change as the research progresses.

■ Ensure that each team member is clear about their role in the team and what tasks are associated with this role.

■ Clarify with all team members that some tasks and roles may overlap and not all will be carried out by only one team member.

■ Decide on authorship of research outputs early on in the process so that each team member can be clear about what to expect from their contribution.

■ Strive to develop effective communication, preferably face-to-face but with the support of electronic media if necessary.

■ Be clear about the amount of time that each team member has available to contribute to the team and that this availability may fluctuate with the demands of other responsibilities they have.

■ Think about how personal and group reflexive practices and awareness can contribute to the cohesion of the team and the quality of the research it conducts.

■ Recognise personal benefits to learning and engagement with a team and how these can enhance your own research practice.

■ Seek to understand other methods and paradigms used in the team by asking questions and incorporating feedback into your own practice.

Further reading

Akerstrom, J., & Brunnberg, E. (2012). Young people as partners in research: Experience from an interactive research circle with adolescent girls. *Qualitative Research, 13*(5), 528–545.

Guest, G., & MacQueen, K. M. (Eds.). (2008). *Handbook for team-based research*. Lanham: AltaMira Press.

Partington, D. (2009). *Essential skills for management research*. London: Sage Publications.

Slatin, C., Galizzi, M., Devereaux Melillo, K., & Mawn, B. (January–February 2004). Conducting interdisciplinary research to promote healthy and safe employment in health care: Promises and pitfalls. *Public Health Reports, 119*, 60–72.

Researching the self, researching one's self

5

'*Cognito ergo sum*'
(*'I am thinking therefore I exist'*)

Descartes, 1644

Chapter map and outcomes

Interest in understanding the human self has existed for centuries, as the famous quote above demonstrates. Whereas previous chapters have discussed using the self to conduct research, this chapter discusses researching both the concept of 'a self' and the research of one's self. Readers will notice as they progress through the chapter that it differs to the other chapters in this book in its concept of 'research'. Rather than research that is focused on hypotheses and experiences, the research discussed in this chapter centres more on understanding the self in relation to professional practice and personal feelings and affect. Research questions are commonly more inward-looking: Who am I? How do I feel? They are asked in order to improve practice: Why am I doing what I do? How can I improve this? Research practice in these arenas differs to socially informed understandings of human behaviour and interaction, centring sometimes on solitary exploration of the self and at other times on sharing deeply personal insight with trusted others.

To help orient the reader to this way of thinking about research, the chapter first discusses the history of research of the self from its early days to contemporary interdisciplinary research practice, to show how humans' interest in being human has been researched for centuries. It then considers the role and place of research of the self in professional practice and considers how advances in technology and computing offer new potential by drawing on biological and technological methods of measurements. It also considers implications of findings to furthering understanding human behaviour and professional practice. The chapter concludes with a discussion of the value of research of the self and some ideas about how it may be conducted. Research examples and researchers' views illustrate key points throughout and tips and strategies for enhancing research of the self are provided at the end.

By the end of the chapter, researchers interested in research of the self will:

- Have an understanding of the history of research of the self
- Know how research of the self can enhance professional practice
- Understand the contribution and the potential for more contribution of technology and computing to research of the self
- Consider how interdisciplinary perspectives on research of the self can contribute to a greater understanding of the self
- Be equipped with practical techniques, knowledge and research designs for conducting research of the self.

Introduction

Researcher View

'I think there's always a set of questions that are fundamentally entangled with yourself, or at least for me about, um, about the relationship between politics, society and self that were in my upbringing.'

The researcher quote above illustrates that interest in the self is deep-rooted and can permeate many research interests. It has been argued that evidence of interest in self can be found in early cave paintings depicting non-physical, psychological selves (Pajares & Schunk, 2002). Early theologians such as Thomas Aquinas were the first to establish the notion of a soul as a separate entity from the body and one that was superior to it. The (written) history of philosophy includes ideas about the self as possessing a physical body and a separate soul. Theorists such as Socrates, Aristotle and Plato described the human soul as a non-material, spiritual aspect of the human self. Descartes was amongst the first philosophers to establish a relationship between the soul and the body by linking 'doubting' with 'thinking'. Spinoza rejected Descartes's distinction between the body and the soul and argued that only one substance exists, making body and soul as one but conceived of in different ways. At the turn of the 20th century, psychology took up an interest in the concept of a self, arguably originating in the inclusion of William James's chapter on 'The Consciousness of Self' in his book *The Principles of Psychology* (1913). In this, the longest chapter in the two-volume book, James differentiated between the self as knower 'I' and the self as known 'Me', with 'Me' being composed of a physical, social and spiritual component. Famously, the introduction by Freud of psychoanalysis and psychoanalytic ideas about separate components of the human psyche led not only to a spawning of new interests in the constitution of the self but also to the development of the psychotherapeutic movement that continues to grow today. Behavioural psychologists such as Bandura advocated the existence of a unitary self that thinks, acts and reflects on its own actions (e.g. Bandura, 1997).

The widespread interest in research to understand the self and associated concepts such as self-esteem, self-efficacy and self-belief has led to the development of contemporary interdisciplinary approaches to its research. Developments in technology and wearable computing allow insight into processes and actions behind actions and decisions. Research conducted between professional and practitioner researchers allows for the impact of understanding the self to be brought to service development and intervention. Understandings of the role of history and context on the constitution of identity enable social and psychological influences to be considered both as separate entities and together as a new psychosocial entity (e.g. Frosh, 2003). Combining approaches in multidisciplinary research is a rapidly emerging focus of interest for researchers of the self.

With these possibilities for insight into the constitution of the self come opportunities for researchers to seek further understanding of the personal meanings of life-changing events, understandings of themselves as practitioners and understandings of themselves as members of communities ('insider' research). Such research differs to research about others because its potential for narcissistic inward-looking subjective insight creates a danger of producing research that is meaningless to others and of little use beyond the development of personal understanding. However, with careful planning, rationale and research design, combined with enhanced self-awareness of the researcher's interest in themselves, research into one's self can contribute new knowledge to minimise personal distress, enable good practice and inform policy and service development whilst also extending the field of understanding of others.

> **Reflective Question:** 'The unexamined life is not worth living' is a well-known quote attributed to Socrates. Do you agree with it? Think about your role in the life you live. How does being you influence and shape what your life entails?

A short history of research of the self

Researcher View

'My parents split up when I was eight and I'm sure that's hugely formative in terms of interests then in intimacy, personal life. You know seeing those sorts of, seeing the residues of all that is in the self that's created and the question about how much you can change, how much you can't. It's a sort of basic question I suppose of sociology and psychosocial studies, you know, what is given and is totally resistant to change and what can be changed. And, you know, my own sort of sense that life was a struggle to reconcile yourself with things that you can change and things that you can't change.'

There are many ways of understanding the self and therefore many ways in which to research it. Researchers of the self have to consider whether they regard the 'self' as a unitary concept or as constructed of different parts. A look at the history of research of the self provides some insight into the ways in which the self has been understood and the ways in which it has been researched over centuries. Descartes's emphasis of the role of inner processes on self-awareness pioneered the notion that mind and body were separate but in a causal relationship and led to the development of **Cartesian dualism**. Cartesian dualism laid the groundwork for subsequent research into the relationships between qualities of experience and qualities of material bodies. Taking up this notion, psychologists and psychoanalysts sought to examine physical disturbances of the body that could not be explained by medical science. One such example is the case of Anna O who consulted Joseph Breuer (1955) with many unexplainable physical symptoms including speech impairment, distorted vision and memory loss. Breuer used Descartes's theory of interactionism to identify that Anna had not sufficiently coped with the death of her father and supressed unwanted feelings, leading to their manifestation as physical symptoms. Talking about her experiences and uncovering the hidden feelings led to the disappearance of the physical symptoms.

Freud took up these ideas from Breuer and developed them extensively into psychoanalysis. Known as the talking cure, Freud developed techniques to encourage distressed patients to talk about their experiences for interpretation by the analyst, enabling access to the pre- and unconscious. Knowing the drives and instincts behind actions and behaviours, as well as an awareness of some of the defence mechanisms that work to obscure difficult and painful feelings, can empower a patient to change and lead a more fulfilling life through the rebalancing of their id, ego and superego. Although disputed by some for the lack of scientific evidence, Freud's work has been powerful in establishing ways of understanding links between mind and body and has led to the development of a vast field of counselling and psychotherapy.

Patients and clients seeking out such support can be seen as researchers of themselves in their quest to know more about why they think and behave in particular ways. Emphasis is also placed on the importance of counsellors, analysts and psychotherapists gaining insight into themselves. With high-quality training in these professions there is an expectation that future practitioners will pursue their own therapy in ongoing research into themselves. They are encouraged to reflect on who they are and consider ways in which they can come to terms with and/or change less palatable or hurtful parts of themselves. In addition to undertaking counselling for themselves, therapists are encouraged to maintain reflective diaries, to consult supervisors to discuss their experiences in the consulting room and to provide peer support about counselling practice to each other.

Reflective Question: Psychotherapy and counselling emphasise and primarily use language to understand how people present themselves and to promote further understanding of the self. What other professions use language to enable others to seek help in gaining knowledge of themselves?

Alongside interest in the language-based approaches to furthering understanding of the self, significant interest in the cognitive and information-processing aspects of human function has developed since the 1980s. These approaches offer the potential to link mind and body in order to develop a more holistic understanding of the self. Cognitive psychologist researchers use advances in technology and computing to explore in detail how coding and de-coding of human thinking, higher-order thinking, memory and problem-solving are carried out. This takes the emphasis away from the personal, emotional and social self toward biological and neurological selves. Findings and implications from such research have been shown to be useful in understanding the self in areas such as academic and employee performance. Identifying motivation to succeed as a key component of performance in these settings initiated a return to understanding aspects of the self, such as self-efficacy and self-esteem (Pajares & Schunk, 2002) and produced evidence that academic performance is directly influenced by how students perceive themselves, their beliefs and their potential. Such findings have placed broader interest in the self back on to research agendas. They have led to the upsurge of interest in teaching roles as well as in promoting self-reflection as part of students' learning and provided an increase in self-study in many professions. Within education, teachers are encouraged to question themselves about their practice by accessing their own beliefs, decisions and motivations to better understand their practice and identify opportunities and ways to improve it.

It is not difficult to understand how interest in this approach to understanding the self has spread to other disciplines such as healthcare, anthropology and sociology. This allows for interdisciplinary research that combines disciplines with newly emerging possibilities for research that include technology and computing. For example, the influence of lifestyle and environment changes can be better understood by combining knowledge about these with knowledge of changes in neural and biological activity of the body. The opportunities afforded by the development of wearable computers that allow for biological measures of, for example, heart rate during activity and sleep. Combining these with audio or written diaries submitted at different points during the day, allow for further understanding of the self.

The chapter next considers the ways in which interdisciplinary research has focused on the self and how these challenge and benefit researchers in this area.

Reflective Question: What apps do you use to measure your biological and emotional changes as you exercise, work and play?

Interdisciplinary approaches to research of the self

Geertz (1975) described the self as 'A bounded, unique, more or less integrated, motivational and cognitive universe' (1975, p. 48). As has been discussed above, this allows for understandings of the self to be sought in a variety of different ways. In addition to biological, physiological and emotional measures of the self in day-to-day contexts the influence of biomedical scientific advances on pre- and post-natal manipulations of the self can also be considered. Genetic alterations and bionic implants are two examples of this.

Researchers now have knowledge of how self-related information is processed in the nervous system (e.g. Keenan et al., in Pajares & Schunk, 2002). The ever-increasing amount of data allows for contemplation of what constitutes the self and calls for a shift in thinking about self-boundaries. Instead of thinking about the self simply in terms of social experience and behaviours, researchers can also consider the role of neural processes. This raises questions about the self and society, the role of culture and the impact of globalisation and technology. Research questions may be better addressed by considering the understanding of the self as an 'ill-defined problem' (Taylor, 1986). According to Taylor (1986), 'ill-defined problems' are those that are ambiguous by necessity and therefore in tension with 'well-defined problems' which have a relatively clear optimal outcome best addressed by 'normal science' (Taylor, 1962). Ill-defined problems can be best addressed using interdisciplinary approaches that allow for the crossing of research boundaries and interaction between researchers (Bruhn, 2000).

RESEARCH EXAMPLE

Summary of research from J. Decety & J. A. Sommerville (2003). Shared representations between self and other: A social cognitive neuroscience view. *Trends in Cognitive Science, 7*(12), 527–533.

The study: This theoretical paper gathers evidence that supports the view of a common representational neural and computational network between self and other from developmental science, social psychology and neuroscience. It challenges the view that sharedness means identicality by arguing that self-awareness and agency are integral components necessary for navigation within shared representations. It locates the inferior parietal cortex and the prefrontal cortex in the right hemisphere of the brain as playing a special role in interpersonal awareness.

Theoretical background: Human survival necessitates abilities to both identify with and distinguish oneself from others through interaction. These researchers conceptualise the self as consisting of several component parts, processes and structures (Neisser, 1988; Robins, Hendin, & Trzesniewski, 2001). They draw on developmental science to understand when and how the self develops, using social and cognitive psychology to understand individuals' knowledge of types of awareness and the potential contents of self-awareness. This has led to identification of early-appearing perceptual forms of the self (ecological and interpersonal selves) which precede more conceptual forms of the self, based on mental representations (Neisser, 1991). It has also led to understanding awareness of the defining features of one's individuality, including awareness of agency over actions and life events, awareness of the distinctiveness of one's life experience, awareness of personal continuity over time and awareness of one's self-reflective capabilities. These researchers point out that awareness of individuality is only possible when comparing self to others and that knowledge of self-attributes is established via comparison with others.

Their study aims to seek a potential role that cognitive neuroscience can play in helping to conceptually define the different dimensions, aspects and characteristics of the self and to address the potential 'separability or relatedness of each component part of self-processing' (p. 528).

Key findings: Developmental science and social psychology suggest that a default mode of the human mind is to view the other like the self. An egocentric bias in the human brain is illustrated in social psychology (Aron, Aron, Tudor, & Nelson, 1991). However it is also necessary to be able to distinguish oneself from the other in order to interact successfully with others. Accepting similar neural representations for self and other behaviour challenges understanding of how self and others' actions are distinguished.

Cognitive-developmental models propose that a single conceptual system is responsible for representation of the self and others' goal-directed actions and have the capacity to co-ordinate first- and third-person information. Key to this is the fact that first-person information is qualitatively different to third-person information and it is this that allows us to distinguish between self and others. Successful integration of these two types of information is essential to successful development and the extent to which imagination and perception are each involved in the generation of these cognitive representations.

Neural research shows that the insula and the right inferior parietal cortex may be crucial in distinguishing the self from the other, evidenced by observing activations in different parts of the brain in response to different stimulations.

Discussion: Findings from developmental science and social psychology show that representations of aspects of the self both overlap with representations of others and are distinct from such representations. Shared representations such as beliefs bring together the cognitive and motivational processes that constitute the contents of culture and so shed light on the self as both special and social, unique and shared. The right hemisphere appears to play a predominant role in the way that self is connected to others, appearing to develop neural activity in the posterior associative

(Continued)

areas earlier than in the left hemisphere. This may underlie infants' capacity to view the other as some way analogous to the self (Hobson, 1989; Meltzoff & Brooks, 2001; Trevarthen, 1979). It seems that the human ability to represent own thoughts and those of others are intimately tied together with similar origins in the brain.

Conclusion: Drawing together the evidence from different disciplinary research approaches to the self provides some insight into new understandings of self-awareness and distinction of self from others. With this it gives rise to new questions such as:

> How can neuroscience and clinical neuroscience help tackle different levels of the self?
> What is the contribution of language and its development in the sense of self?

For full details and a list of questions for further research, see Decety & Sommerville (2003) referenced above.

This study shows how bringing together different foci of brain activity can illuminate less-measurable aspects of the human mind, such as self-awareness. It draws on the disciplinary expertise of each approach and combines findings to propose new ways of understanding aspects of human function and to raise new questions for future research.

Thinking about this in terms of researching *one's self* poses further challenges. Most researchers are trained within one discipline and the knowledge they have and seek is derived from that discipline. However, considering the many ways in which disciplines can interact may help when considering the possibilities of researching one's self.

There are a number of approaches that combine disciplinary perspectives to research the self, as shown in the box below.

DISCIPLINARY PERSPECTIVES

Cross-disciplinarity: can be understood to draw on different disciplines with different levels of interaction. Thus a researcher who is an educational psychologist may be interested in understanding themselves in terms of their professional practice. They can do this by exploring their performance in terms of their beliefs and the demands of their profession. The outcome of their research may emphasise either their performance or their role, depending on why they are conducting the research into themselves.

Interdisciplinarity: can be understood as creating a theoretical, methodological and conceptual identity by reaching common ground and drawing on each component equally. If the educational psychologist researcher is seeking understanding of themselves in their professional context they may wish to disseminate the findings in a publication or conference presentation that provides a detailed overview of the study for use by others.

Transdisciplinarity: calls for an integration of disciplinary epistemologies. The educational psychologist researching themselves in order to better understand their professional performance may encounter issues and topics that do not fit neatly into their discipline, such as the role of cognition in addressing administrative tasks. They may seek to blend this understanding into their existing knowledge in an effort to challenge their pre-suppositions and extend the categorised discipline-based knowledge.

Rogers, Scaife and Rizzo (2005) state that cross-disciplinary work most commonly takes place within the researcher's home discipline in which available theoretical frameworks, methods and concepts are adapted and modified to reach a new understanding. This is likely to also necessitate drawing on ideas from outside the discipline and therefore requires of the sole researcher researching themselves an openness to other ways of understanding and seeking knowledge.

In the next section this chapter considers ways of researching the self in relation to professional practice. It demonstrates the value of doing this, some of the challenges and some of the pitfalls with the use of a model designed to support this approach.

Self-research and professional practice

The value of researching one's self can perhaps be most clearly understood by considering it in relation to professional practice. It enables the self-researcher to define the parameters of their inquiry, to generate new knowledge about themselves and those they work with and to consider themselves within the specific professional environment in which they work. It allows them to ask questions about their own practice, to pursue particular problems they encounter and to follow the threads of particular issues that interest them in their professional environment. The value of studying one's self lies in its potential for constructive critique and many say that this is further enhanced by collaborative processes, exemplified by the establishment of learning communities in which engaged scholarship with others promotes dialogue and collective cognition (Murphy, Dempsey, & Halton, 2010). One way that this is promoted is through the establishment of the support of **critical friends**.

A critical friend is 'a term coined by Kemmis and McTaggart (1988) to denote a person who will listen to a researcher's account of practice and critique the thinking behind the account' (Whitehead & McNiff, 2006, p. 256). Critical friends are often trusted colleagues with whom self-researchers can gain ongoing support to discuss and query personal understandings in their quest to gain new perspectives on personal interpretations of themselves and their practice. Through this process of personal-situated inquiry the research of one's self can be formalised with an ethos of trust and development.

A methodological framework of self-study for teachers has been developed by Samaras (2011), who has drawn on the work of Barnes (1998), LaBoskey (2004), Loughran and Northfield (1998) and Samaras and Freese (2006) to develop the Five Foci Model (Samaras, 2010), which provides a methodological framework made up of five components to enable self-study by teachers.

Summary of the Five Foci Model from A. P. Samaras (2010). *Self-study teacher research: Improving your practice through collaborative inquiry.* **Sage Publications Inc.**

Personal-situated inquiry: allows teachers to draw on personal experience from within their classroom to generate their own research questions from the observations they have made. It provides opportunity to examine lived practice and to seek out living contradictions between what the researcher says and what they do. Exploring this gap creates new understandings of personal theory-making.

Critical collaborative inquiry: is a personal and interpersonal inquiry into learning, thinking and knowing. Knowledge is acquired through the questioning of and listening to divergent views and alternative perspectives that help with the validation of the quality and legitimation of each other's claims.

Improved learning: to learn what works, what does not work and the consequences of changes brought about by the research of themselves in their professional practice.

A transparent and systematic process: that requires openness, honesty and clear descriptions of spirals of questioning, framing and reframing of interpretations and revisiting of data.

Knowledge generation and presentation: although focused on the self, the purpose of much self-study is to contribute not only to a personal knowledge base but to the professional knowledge base, too. This enables wider review and critique and the opportunity to build validation across related work.

The framework shows that self-study goes beyond only studying one's self in processes of reflection that draw only on personal knowledge to consider how understanding of one's own thinking and practices can enhance the learning of students. The self-study researcher is an insider who is able to use themselves as an instrument of the research and make explicit the inherent assumptions brought to practice (Mason, 2002). Thus a key pitfall of undertaking self-study may be the mistaken assumption that it is always conducted alone. Even if the focus is on one's self, and one's own practice, self-study benefits from the support of others, here in the form of critical friends, with whom the research of the self can be queried and the research process and its outcomes discussed, also enabling a dialogue over different perspectives brought to it and its interpretations.

The following research example illustrates some of the challenges of a 'critical friend' approach and how these can be overcome:

RESEARCH EXAMPLE

Summary taken from a wider study: S. Schunk & T. Russell (2005). Self-study, critical friendship and the complexities of teacher education. *Studying Teacher Education*, *1*(2), 107–121.

The study: Two teacher educators, one based in Canada (Russell) and one based in Australia (Schunk), agreed to act to develop a critical friend relationship when Russell was asked to take over three secondary science method classes midway through an eight-month programme.

Methodology: Experiences in the classroom were shared by email on a weekly basis with the critical friend over a five-week period. The teacher wrote notes each week to email to the critical friend for comments and questions, using the understanding that a critical friend critiques existing practices to enable their own rethinking and reframing of practice (Loughran & Northfield, 1998).

Findings: The researchers found that having a critical friend forced them to maintain a reflective journal and to document their experiences when they might not have done so otherwise. Both found having a critical friend beneficial to gaining insight into their teaching practice – both by giving and by receiving constructive feedback that led to insight and change in their practice.

By participating as a critical friend the researchers reported learning the critical elements of trust, flexibility and support as essential to the process. Frank and comprehensive discussion of roles were also found to be key to the value of the relationship.

With this came challenges arising from practical aspects such as not being able to have face-to-face discussions when they were in separate

(Continued)

countries and the impact of status, in which a critical friend to a more senior colleague found it challenging to know how much they could say. This was addressed sometimes by adopting a more passive role that offered support and encouraging reflection rather than actively questioning and provoking practice.

Both researchers found that the process of thinking and writing about practice may have been more valuable than reading the critical friend's reactions to the practice.

The researchers identified strong parallels between students learning to teach and the process of learning to be critical friends.

Discussion: The study highlights a number of ways in which the critical friend process could have been improved. The researchers identified the greatest constraints as being time and communicating electronically. Using only a short course of seven weeks' duration and not being able to discuss aspects of the process and its findings in greater depth meant that some issues were not explored fully or were overlooked completely.

The researchers recommend having a frank and thorough discussion before the start of the critical friend process so that the expectations and concerns of both parties can be considered, particularly in light of differences in status of each person.

The researchers also suggest that the practitioner examining their own work can feed back to the critical friend how their needs are being met, enabling the critical friend to both learn from the experience and improve practice as a critical friend.

The study presents a number of conclusions which highlight that personal friendships and shared assumptions about teacher education are not guarantees of a successful critical friendship and that the critical friend expects benefits as well as the person whose teaching is being studied. The necessity of allowing sufficient time for the process to unfold sensitively is essential and context is central to the understanding of practice. This means that discussion of context should precede and support observations and discussion of teaching. The role of risk in the friendship is highlighted. The researchers conclude that 'self study is an inherently critical activity that seeks to challenge one's fundamental assumptions about personal professional practice' (p. 120). This means that in order for self-study to be valuable the critical friend must be prepared and enabled to take risks and be as critical as possible to reduce the likelihood of neglecting relevant data and perspectives.

This example shows that although a valuable learning experience, self-study through dialogue with others brings the personal to the process in ways that can be challenging and threatening. The need to develop such study sensitively is key to its likelihood of success.

> **Reflective Question**: What are the risks of sharing insights into yourself with others? Think about the personal, professional and interrelational threats and benefits that can come from doing so.

In addition to offering a research process that is empowering and places the practitioner researcher at the centre of the inquiry, research of the self demands a self-reflective stance to sit alongside a responsibility to self and others. It brings an accountability for one's practice both to oneself and to others in the profession but it also demands that those under observation are prepared to hear criticism, and challenges to their assumptions about themselves and their teaching practice.

The next section describes a method of self-study that explicitly calls on researchers to increase awareness of their own practice in order to create opportunities for change in it.

The 'Discipline of Noticing'

The Discipline of Noticing (Mason, 2002) is a methodical and systematic approach to enhancing practice first devised for use by teachers to inform and improve their practice but applicable to many professionals working with people. It capitalises on the 'sporadic and serendipitous noticing' (Mason, 2002, p. 63) of everyday practice by suggesting ways in which professionals can become more sensitive to noticing opportunities in the moment. The approach suggests:

Keeping accounts
Developing sensitivities
Recognising choices
Preparing and noticing
Labelling
Validating with others (Mason, 2002).

As such, this approach regards noticing as research and places the researcher's research of their own practice at its centre. It takes as its central tenet the researcher's awareness of what they are attending to and the breadth and limitations of their attention. The aim of this disciplined noticing is the question of how to stimulate others to attend to aspects that will be of benefit to them. The approach is supported with a range of exercises, which range from working alone and developing accounts and questions about one's own practice to working with others to query and validate the observations and the moments of observations identified. The outcome aims to be an enhanced awareness of where opportunities for beneficial change in practice may lie.

The approach raises interesting questions about validity when researching one's self. Recognising that validity is an important aspect of research (although subjective researchers may prefer the term 'trustworthiness') Mason asks 'If I am observing myself, how can I be sure that I am not fooling myself, much less convince someone else of this?' (p. 187). To address this issue Mason proposes that it is the development of an inner monitor that enables professionals to become experts that can modify their actions by intuition and expert sensitivities.

The Discipline of Noticing offers individuals behavioural training and education in awareness in order to achieve this inner monitor. The following example provides an illustration of how this works in practice.

RESEARCH EXAMPLE

Summary of research from S. Breen et al. (2011). Reflection in practice: The Discipline of Noticing. In C. Smith (Ed.), *Proceedings of the British Society for Research into Learning Mathematics*, Vol. 31(3), November 2011.

The study: A group of mathematics lecturers drawn from five higher education institutions in Ireland conducted a study to reflect on their own teaching using the Discipline of Noticing approach. Each lecturer wrote accounts of critical incidents that occurred in their classes using the approach guidelines to keep them as free from opinion and value judgements as possible. Accounts were shared and analysed amongst the group in regular meetings throughout an academic year. At the end of the year the challenges and benefits to students and teachers were identified and reflected upon.

Study aims: The study had four key aims:

To become aware on an individual level of what was happening in the classroom

To recognise more easily the opportunities to act differently in the classroom and so to improve teaching

To further inform good teaching practice by meeting regularly with colleagues to discuss the accounts

To enable identification of various phenomena in undergraduate teaching.

Methodology: Each lecturer wrote 'brief but vivid' accounts of incidents in their classes each week, according to Mason's proposal that accounts of incidents should be given 'without explanation, justification or emotive terms' (Mason, 2002, p. 40) in order to distinguish between an 'account of', which describes an event as objectively as possible minimising evaluation and judgement, and to 'account for', which offers interpretation, explanation, value judgement or criticism. The basis for this approach is that whilst events that stay in memory are usually imbued with emotional or intellectual commitment, they cannot be analysed unless impartial clarity about what they consist of is first achieved.

The accounts were circulated to all members of the group every three weeks and the group met twice per semester to discuss them. This builds on findings that discussion, sharing and challenging of similar observations by groups of people reduces the likelihood of practices stagnating (Mason, 2002).

At the end of the academic year, each lecturer described and considered the process of reflecting on their practice in this way. The descriptions were coded and categorised by one participant and discussed by the group.

Key findings: The lecturers found it challenging to both notice and continue the flow of their teaching at the outset of the study. Mason distinguishes between 'noticing' to make a distinction, 'marking' to be able to make mention of what has been noticed and 'recording' to make a note of what has been noticed in order to re-mark on it later. These lecturers found it easier to reflect on a lesson after it had been completed than to interrupt its evolution by setting themselves to 'notice' and 'mark' critical incidents during it. They found that at times they were left thinking that nothing of note had happened during the lesson or that more mundane lessons provided more time for 'noticing'.

The lecturers found that contextual factors such as group size and familiarity with student cohorts influenced their practice. They found that it was easier to mark incidents occurring in smaller groups than in larger groups and that it was easier to establish the discipline of noticing and marking with those cohorts with whom they met more regularly.

The support of the collaborative group was reported by all the lecturers as being invaluable. Setting deadlines for submission of accounts and knowing that they would be shared helped to establish a regular discipline of reflection.

The formal forum provided by the regular group meetings enabled the lecturers to learn about different teaching styles. This pooling of experience offered great potential for professional development.

The discipline of the attempts to step back from practice in order to notice and record incidents enabled clearer articulation of concerns and issues in the accounts. This approach also helped to identify themes permeating through accounts, allowing clearer identification of personal teaching styles.

The Discipline of Noticing proved to be a process that required practice and the implementation of a structure of accountability for these lecturers. They were compelled to address the initial tensions to maintain a coherent and flowing teaching style during their lessons whilst also seeking to attend to their inner monitor and carry out recording tasks. The study shows that it was often easier to record incidents after the lesson than during it and that, consequently, most reflection was carried out not in the moment, as required by the approach, but following it. However, the support and opportunity for sharing offered by the collaborative nature of the study design provided rich insight and knowledge not only of each individual's personal professional practice but also commonalities that may be usefully disseminated to the wider mathematics teaching community.

It can be seen that two key ways of researching one's self, that of self-study using the Five Foci Model and the Discipline of Noticing, are based on consultation and collaboration with others. These allow contribution of constructive querying and critique of individual interpretations of practice, leading to improvement and opportunities to institute change and also for the identification and learning of common themes within different people's practice, allowing for validation and contribution to the wider profession.

In the next sections of this chapter, the focus will be on self-research approaches that are carried out in more solitary fashion: those of reflexive writing and self-monitoring with technology. Each section will describe the ways in which these approaches to researching the self have developed over recent years, their potential for application to a range of interests in understanding the self and ways in which such research can be carried out.

Writing as reflection in research of the self

Researcher View

'There was a real problem there that I needed to understand but it was a complex problem and I struggled writing that paper for a long time. So what did I enjoy? I enjoyed getting to the end of it. [Laughs]. Not having to work on it anymore. But I enjoyed a sense of satisfaction. I felt like I had really grappled with something that was difficult and that was kind of profoundly psychosocial that was both really about the original research question but was also pushing my work in a bit of a new direction. And maybe see something about myself. You know it clarified, it brought to the fore I suppose, just how much it can matter if you let go of where you are emotionally at the time you're doing the research.'

Writing has been divided into scientific and literary writing since the 17th century (Richardson, 2002). Broadly speaking, scientific writing presents facts and objectivity; fiction is associated with subjectivity and rhetoric. Commonly, quantitative research is written to report details of the inquiry and to portray the researcher as a witness to it through description of scientific studies and presentation of evidence of the results. Qualitative research write-ups make explicit the subjective experience and the researcher's role in the research. New styles of research writing and the use of different genres of writing such as 'creative non-fiction' (Caulley, 2008) and 'Grab' (Glaser, 1978) have emerged in efforts to enthral the reader and enliven qualitative research writing: 'Grab' by presenting 'interesting and memorable' material that clearly links the study to theoretical concepts (Gilgun, 2005) and 'creative non-fiction' by using fiction techniques to write non-fiction that remains close to the study data.

It is recognised that the qualitative research write-up is a method of inquiry itself (Janesick, 2000). It allows the researcher to examine and consider their relationship with the topic and to show the audience how this has shaped and influenced the research. By illustrating the co-construction of the research through involvement of participants and researchers, the reader is invited to contribute further to the process through the openness of the relationship formed with them. Interweaving of researcher and participant voices and the inclusion of anecdotes, poetry and metaphors work to bring the research context to the reader. Interactive forms of research writing invite feedback from the reader and extend the research process (Grbich, 2007).

Understanding writing as both a product and a process (Colyar, 2009) allows insight into the meaning and use of other linguistic features such as silence and non-words in the representation of research. Van Manen (1990) proposes that in order for the text to achieve a certain effect on its reader it can be important to leave some things unsaid. If a researcher is unable to access the language and concepts referred to by the participants, the inclusion of direct quotes from them can play an important role. Participants' silence about topics or experiences can be more telling to a researcher than attempts to elicit responses from them (Van Manen, 1990, p. 113). For the researcher as author, the inclusion of non-words that symbolise memory-joggers, unvocalised meanings and cues to recall in drafts and rewrites can be an important part of the research process (Colyar, 2009). Although usually edited out in the final presentation, their inclusion in the drafts leaves their mark on the final style and content of the research write-up.

These forms of writing can be considered as reflections on the research process that also address a key quality criteria of qualitative research: reflexivity. Reflexivity demonstrates an awareness by the researcher of the influence of their role in the research process, the role of the method selected to carry it out and the role of the epistemology used to identify what constitutes knowledge and how it can be obtained. However, these forms of writing are oriented towards an eventual audience. They are written (or at least presented) with the audience in mind and sometimes according to criteria demanded by journals or academic assessors.

Reflective Question: What are some of the issues that may prevent or inhibit you from engaging in reflective writing? Think about getting started, what you might find yourself writing about and the effects of coming to know things about yourself that you did not know before.

In the next section the chapter considers writing reflexively to further the understanding of one's self.

Writing as reflection in research of one's self

Writing reflexively is about using the writing process to reflect on what you are writing about. Although it is a term that conjures up images of reflective calm, writing reflexively can be a dynamic and fast-moving process leading to insights and understandings about personal questions of 'how' and 'why'. There may be some conscious realisations about one's self, arising from the process as well as some insight into your relationship to the research. The challenges of writing reflexively and of writing about self-reflexivity can range from finding words to convey feelings through to concerns about exposing personal experiences but an attractive aspect of writing reflexively in research of the self is that this writing may never need to be seen by an audience. One such approach is 'through the mirror' writing (Bolton, 2010).

'Through the mirror' writing as reflection

'Through the mirror' writing is a reflective practice that aids writers to construct reality through creative exploration. It aims to 'facilitate a wider view from a distance, close acute observation, authority over practice, and a critical challenging attitude to assumptions about diversity of perspective, and taken-for-granteds about political, social and cultural norms' (Bolton, 2011, p. 85). 'Through the mirror' writing requires the writer to take responsibility for their own learning and writing by screening out unwanted reflections by using a process of high concentration. Its benefits are the discovery of previously unknown thoughts, knowledge and understandings, all of which can contribute to a greater insight into the self and personal practices and actions. Its challenges are the potential for risk, play and loss of sense and meaning (Flax, 1990, p. 192). Reflexive writing is a form of dialogue with the self that enables multi-perspectival thinking. This frees the writer from constraints of linking meanings and concepts for an audience and provides a creative process of exploration. In turn, this can enable the writer to write separately for an audience with confidence and authority.

'Through the mirror' writing regards content as the most important aspect and has little concern for grammar and other 'rules of writing'. It develops uncensored, unjudged and noncritical narratives that no one else need ever see. The writer is regarded as having authority over their own expression and of only ever writing pieces that are right and written for the self. Of most importance is the process and not the product of 'through the mirror' writing.

Bolton (2011) suggests five stages of 'through the mirror' writing:

Five stages of 'through the mirror' writing

Stage 1: The six-minute write
This stage aims to allow the writer to clear their mind of unwanted thoughts and questions by writing them out and thereby freeing the mind to follow its own track.

Stage 2: The story
Without thinking about grammar, spelling or other rules of writing the writer should write a story of experience immediately after the six-minute write. The story can be about anything that comes to mind and is best written without rereading the six-minute write to avoid responsive thinking interrupting the flow of writing the story.

Stage 3: Read and respond
Reading one's writing back to oneself creates a dialogue with the self and can lead to additional writing of responses that are provoked by it. Questions may arise about why particular aspects of the six-minute write or the story are surprising or puzzling. Writers can ask

themselves questions about the language they have used or contradictions that may have been written into the story.

Stage 4: Sharing the writing with a peer
Depending on why the 'through the mirror' writing process is being engaged, this stage may or may not be pursued. If a researcher is seeking to understand an aspect of their practice they may benefit from sharing the writing with a trusted colleague who can perceive wider institutional contexts. If the writing is part of self-exploration relating to personal and private experience, the writer may not wish to share what they have written when accessing their inner self.

Stage 5: Developing writing
In this stage the writer seeks to deepen and widen understanding by asking questions such as 'What would it be like if...?' or by considering different endings to the story by writing as the other. This may entail writing thought bubbles for puzzling characters that have appeared in the story or rewriting the story with the control placed in a different person's hands.

The usefulness of 'through the mirror' writing to understanding more about one's self can be seen in its potential to tap into previously obscured thoughts or forgotten memories. Agency is placed in the writer's hands in a safe manner that allows personal and creative exploration until a satisfactory end point is reached. This may be particularly useful when trying to make sense of experiences of research into sensitive topics or to understand self-perceptions of others' behaviour. This might be research into child abuse or experiences of being bullied at work for example. A thoughtful piece by Lubna Chaudhry (Chaudhry, 1997) is written as a personal narrative presented as 'fragments of a reflexive tale' in which she explores with the reader her positionality as a Pakistani Muslim researcher affiliated with a US institution and conducting ethnographic research with Pakistani Muslim immigrants in California. This non-traditional form of writing for a journal (*Qualitaive Studies in Education*) carefully and provocatively leads the reader through the questions, concerns, and conflicts that this researcher has in interactions with Muslims, non-Muslims, family members and research participants and their families. It does not present 'Findings' in the usual journal article style but instead the narrative is peppered with insights and unanswered questions that both address some of the issues and raise others in collaboration with the reader.

> ### Researcher View
>
> 'I think although this is an impossible task, I would say struggle to know yourself. The idea that you can research the selves of others without having some engagement with understanding yourself is a false position. And is a kind of othering, you know I will research the selves of others but no one will need to know about me, you know that's irrelevant. So I would say that you, if you're interested in the self, you've got to read theoretically around different ways of understanding the self, but you also need to put some investment of time and energy into some sorts of kind of self-exploration, self-interrogation. I'm not saying everyone needs to go into therapy or psychoanalysis necessarily, but I think that certainly helps. But the idea that you can understand the selves of others without understanding your own self or try to understand yourself and I think I would also say you can only ever try to understand both yourself and the selves of others, because selves are incredibly complex and not knowable. So there I would sort of accept something fundamental that psychoanalysis has to say which is that there are elements of selves in subjectivities that constantly elude knowing and fixing and we have to have a kind of humility about that. We can't think that we can fully research any self or fully understand selves.'

The section above has shown how the subjectivity of reflexive writing can be harnessed and valued in pursuit of further understanding of the self. As was described at the start of this chapter, there are other ways in which the self is being researched and understood that use advances in technology, neuroscience and biological measurement. These apparently primarily objective approaches enable different insights into the constitution of the self, whilst also relying on participants adopting a self-research perspective through their engagement with wearable technology and diary-keeping. It is to this that the next section of this chapter turns.

Wearable computing

The rapid upsurge in development and ownership of mobile smartphones in the last decade provides myriad opportunities for data gathering about the self through social networking, wearable and embedded sensors and audio and visual recordings. The mobile phone provides a forum for self-expression, social learning and role exploration (Morris & Aguilera, 2012) often in ways that are unobtrusive, anonymous (to an extent) and accessible to many. The number of worldwide broadband subscribers is expected to reach 900 million by the end of 2018 (http://point-topic.com/free-analysis/five-year-broadband-subscriber-forecasts-to-end-2018/). It has been found that in Japan the mobile phone is experienced as an extension to the self (Ito, Daisuke, & Matuda, 2006). Lindstrom (2011) reports that users respond to the iPhone sound as they do to a loved one at the neural level (Lindstrom, 2011) and Barkhuus and Polichar (2011) report that the powerful multi-functionality of the typical smartphone makes it an all-in-one lifestyle technology akin to a Swiss army penknife (Barkhuus & Polichar, 2011 in Miller, 2012).

The possibilities for research offered by mobile technology range from large-scale worldwide studies to multi-perspective case studies for individuals. Its use allows for study of physiological and biological behaviours in different contexts and whilst carrying out different activities (ranging from sleep to physical exercise) for assessment about functioning in everyday life and for self-monitoring and study. Runyan et al. (2013) describe how use of an app to collect real-time data from students led to an increased self-awareness of how they spend their time. The development of wearable sensors places less emphasis on the participant to actively input data and instead relies on passive tracking of physiological responses, movement and location.

One example of a wearable sensor is the Jawbone UP®. This is a bracelet which senses activity and physical states from a wristband and provides feedback on diet, sleep and exercise (Morris & Aguilera, 2012). There are also head-worn sensors that identify brain activity. Reduction of back pain can be achieved through the use of posture sensors that are integrated with pain-management interventions (Morris & Aguilera, 2012).

Mobile technologies can be of great use and importance to researchers seeking to gather large data sets of information about others. They can also offer valuable ways to individuals to assess their own states of emotional and biological well-being. This makes them of value to practitioners, too, and an increasing number of therapists are developing and using technologically based ways for clients to enhance their therapeutic interventions.

One such example is the Beating the Blues programme (www.beatingtheblues.co.uk) which offers sufferers of depression and anxiety support and help to understand the link between how they think and how this influences their feelings and behaviours. It is based on cognitive behavioural therapy techniques and principles recommended by the National Institute of Health and Care Excellence and used by GPs, both for its efficacy and to reduce the costs of face-to-face meetings with patients. In addition to offering a way for its users to research and understand themselves, technological support such as this provides access to support in the privacy of users' homes, meaning that the stigma of approaching professionals for help may be reduced.

The rise in the development of mobile phone applications (apps) has led to a huge range of apps designed for individuals to research themselves. Many are related to physical and mental health. Amongst the most popular health and fitness apps currently available in Apple's App Store (https://itunes.apple.com/gb/genre/ios-health-fitness/id6013?mt=8&letter=M&page=12#page) are

Fitness Buddy: 1700+ workout and fitness exercises
My Diet Diary
Lifesum: Lifestyle tracker and calorie counter
Digipill: Sleep, relaxation and mindfulness
Smoke Free: Quit smoking now and stop for good.

Those related to mood-tracking include 'MoodPanda: Mood diary and mood tracker' and 'MoodMinder', advertised as 'the collaboration between a clinical psychiatrist and programmer'.

These give just a flavour of all that is available to an individual looking to track themselves and doubtless there are many more available on other mobile platforms. In the research example below, an exploratory study was conducted to examine the potential of mobile phone technologies to broaden access to cognitive behavioural therapy and to provide in-the-moment support to users.

RESEARCH EXAMPLE

Research summary from M. E. Morris et al. (2010). Mobile therapy: Case study evaluations of a cell phone application for self-awareness. *Journal of Medical Internet Research*, *12*(2), e10.

Participants: Eight participants who had reported significant stress during an employee health assessment were recruited. The study reports a case study of one participant who had been coping with longstanding marital conflict.

Methodology: The researchers developed a mobile phone application with touchscreen single-dimension scales for self-reporting of moods, a mood map, therapeutic exercises for cognitive reappraisals designed to examine maladaptive interpretations, and physical relaxation. Participants were prompted via their mobile phones to report their moods several

(Continued)

times a day. Weekly open-ended interviews were held with each participant over a month-long period to discuss their use of the device and to respond to longitudinal views of the data.

Analysis: Interview narratives were thematically analysed and mood changes assessed over the course of the study. The mobile data was interrogated based on stressful incidents reported in the interviews.

Case study results: The participant noticed a drop in energy each evening and began practising relaxation therapies on his phone each day before entering his house. His mean anger, anxiety and stress ratings were lower in the second half of the study than in the first half after initiation of the techniques (*P* less than or equal to 0.1 for all three scales).

Discussion: In weekly interviews all participants showed understanding of the mood scales and responded to them in a way that was generally consistent with self-reflection. The data showed personal improvement over the course of the study and during stressful episodes.

Conclusion: The mood mapping and therapeutic concepts were quickly grasped by the participants and they applied them creatively to help themselves and to empathise with others. This is seen as a non-stigmatising way to increase access to personal therapy and to provide access to therapy for those who would not otherwise have it.

This example shows that individuals are able and willing to research themselves with apps designed for access throughout the day. The research can lead to self-intervention or inform intervention design by others. The self-researcher is empowered to take control in understanding and addressing aspects of themselves identified these ways, and as in this study the effects can be beneficial to the individual and to their interactions with others.

Particularly useful to providing non-stigmatising empowering mental healthcare, research of the self using technology can also draw on the stages of the therapeutic alliance traditionally developed in face-to-face meetings to improve research of the self and intervention. Miller (2012) suggests using the qualities of trust, empathy and collaborative investigation to inform the interaction design and capabilities of these technologies. Clinicians can promote optimal engagement with the tools by patients by helping them to become more sophisticated in their use of them and by providing feedback to developers. However, she also recognises a greater challenge in these technologies to develop interpretations that can further assist patients to raise insight and ability to recognise choices.

Using the example of an app that goes beyond hearing and fulfilling demands by responding simply to questions asked of it, Miller proposes developments of apps that offer further questions about the questioner's values and long-term goals. Whilst she acknowledges that this needs to be done carefully in order not to test the patience and mental health of the questioner, she argues that the qualities required to build an alliance can be integrated with a range of other psychological principles in order to help individuals make sustained changes in their lives. Integrating the technology capable of this into the therapeutic relationship can make the patient feel cared for even through prompts and messages from a therapist that are automated.

However Miller flags up some limitations and challenges to this form of research, too. Risks of data loss or insufficient memory space, battery power and dissemination of heat generated from the use of mobile phones more frequently and in different ways for which they were designed are present and call for prioritising of these issues in developing the potential for their use this way. It is important to remember that some geographical locations do not yet have broadband access and some people are excluded by their socio-economic circumstances from owning mobile phones. Similarly, some older people may not be willing to learn how to use the apps. Participants' behaviour may constrain the research so that they may lose interest in the study or forget to carry or charge their phones. Whilst this may be less of a possibility for those participants seeking to research themselves, it has serious implications for the data collection. As in all research, participants may change their behaviour because they know they are being researched (even by themselves).

Knowledge about how to programme apps is limited for those who do not work in the technology field. It seems possible that some disciplines such as psychology may begin to offer courses on app development in order to further research methodologies. The rapid rise of app technology and use calls for new forms of data management and storage that will safely record, organise, analyse and interpret large volumes of data. Concerns about the ethical issues of such research continue to mount. Recently, in the UK, a government plan for the collection of electronic data on patient care from GPs had to be shelved in response to widespread concern from citizens about privacy and anonymity (BBC News, 2014). It is hard to collect thoughtful informed consent from smartphone studies and the GP data-collection plan was criticised in relation to this for having an opt-out approach rather than an opt-in one. It may be that anonymity will gradually become impossible in data-rich smartphone studies (King, 2011). Also that even with encrypted data uploads and privacy-preserving data analysis, confidentiality will be vulnerable to authorities. With current awareness of the monitoring of texts and emails by those concerned to prevent terrorism, researchers seeking to conduct research using technology may be wary of who may be viewing their personal data.

Nonetheless, advances in technologies offer new possibilities for research of the self by inviting self-tracking of mental and physical health and by identifying contextual variables associated with life-style. The possibilities for individuals to understand themselves and their needs as a result of their self-research, allows for their direct contribution to tailor-mad or generalised therapeutic intervention.

It seems most appropriate to end this chapter with a researcher's view of the challenges of researching the self:

Researcher View

'I think there's a challenge around the legitimacy of it, about whether it's either other people's selves or yourself as the researcher. But especially of yourself and the researcher that there's a kind of sense in which it could be seen as a narcissistic exercise, you know, totally wrapped up in your own self and losing sense of the wider world. And even being interested in the selves of others is seen I think by many social scientists, many sociologists as being middle class you know, you've got the luxury to worry about the self, while most people still don't have enough food to eat. It would be seen as a kind of Western, middle-class luxury to think about the self. So I think there's still quite, there are very strong kind of politicised beliefs about that that I certainly find get under my skin, maybe because I suppose there's an element of truth in it. But only an element of truth in it, because actually selves are overwhelming and experiences of mental distress and, um, you know If yourself, if the self is not reasonably comfortable, reasonably stable, reasonably okay, then the rest of life is impossible. So I don't think that it's only Western, middle-class people who have selves and I don't think it's only Western middle-class people who struggle with their selves. But I think that kind of discourse is difficult and so I find difficult the sort of sense that it's an indulgence and that it's a deviation from the real matters of kind of material living. That's probably for me the biggest thing, the kind of political objection to it, which I think is wrong, but does get under my skin.'

Chapter summary

This chapter has considered different ways of understanding and exploring the self and the value of combining interdisciplinary approaches to gain new insight and directions for future research.

The chapter has acknowledged the broad interest in the human self and distinguished between researching the self and researching one's self. It has highlighted the importance of recognising the strengths and limitations, alongside the interest and motivations of self-research and linked these to professional practice and performance enhancement. The chapter has outlined some of the new possibilities in research of the self, available through advances in technological and computational developments. It identifies the topicality of these approaches as these fields rapidly develop. Self-researchers are positioned to consider and learn more about research outside of their own field and that which is available to them in new fields of measurement, assessment and intervention.

Hints and tips

- Think about the perspective you are bringing to your research. Is it based on an academic discipline, interest in personal experience and/or desire to assess your professional performance?
- Consider the strengths and limitations of the perspective you are bringing. What aspects of the self does it enable you to explore? What will not be accessible to this perspective?
- Address the skills and knowledge gap in your approach. What additional methods, measurements or perspectives will enable the research to be extended? How can you access these?
- What is your motivation for wanting to know more about the self? Is it personal, professional or academic? How will each of these impact on the way that the research is carried out?
- Learn about up-and-coming ways of researching the self. What can new technology contribute to the study? How can you acquire the skills and knowledge needed to use these approaches?
- Write about the experience of conducting research into the self, even if it is not research into yourself. The value of a reflective stance in research has been shown to enhance the research process, the experience of the research process and the outcomes of it.
- Remember that research into the self is usually not conducted by oneself but requires peer support, often in the form of critical friendships.
- Be clear about what methodological and theoretical frameworks you are bringing to the research. This may be easier to do when researching others but is even more important when researching yourself, in order to minimise subjective biasing and obscuration of relevant data.

Further reading

Brackenridge, C. (1999). Managing myself: Investigator survival in sensitive research. *International Review for the Sociology of Sport, 34*(4), 399–410.

Breen, C. (2000). Re-searching teaching: Changing paradigms to improve practice. In K. Clements, H. Tairab, & W. Yoong (Eds.), *Science, mathematics and technical education in the 20th and 21st centuries.* Brunei: University Brunei Darussalam.

Day, E. (2002). Me, My*self and I: Personal and professional re-constructions in ethnographic research. *Forum: Qualitaitve Social Research, 3*(3), Art. 11.

Hobbs, D., & May, T. (Eds.). (1993). *Interpreting the field.* Oxford: Oxford University Press.

McCartan, C., Schubotz, D., & Murphy, J. (2012). The self-conscious researcher- post-modern perspectives of participatory research with young people. *Forum: Qualitative Social Research, 13*(1), Art. 9.

Researcher identity: prospects and challenges

6

Chapter map and outcomes

This final chapter returns to some of the key themes of the book to evaluate and draw them together in a final consideration of the researcher role. By considering researcher positionality and ways in which researchers can be research instruments in different forms of research and in different contexts, as discussed in chapters 2 and 3, it presents some conclusions about the constitution of researcher identity. It then provides some strategies for researchers and users of research to raise their awareness of researcher identity and how the researcher influences and can shape the research process. Next, it discusses how researchers can effectively conduct research with different paradigmatic differences when researching alone and when researching with other researchers. The chapter asks to what extent expertise in being both an objective and a subjective researcher can be reached and, finally, poses questions about what challenges lie at the heart of research practice when considering the role of the researcher. The chapter ends by discussing next steps in the consideration of understanding and implementing awareness of the researcher role into research. Throughout the chapter, the reader is asked to consider questions relevant to their own research and encouraged to raise questions of their own that will assist them in improving understanding of their researcher role. By doing so, it helps researchers to improve the quality of all the research they conduct and to effectively critique the research of others.

Having read this chapter, readers will:

■ Be able to collate ideas, queries and concerns about awareness of the researcher role

- Have identified key aspects of the research role that have been identified in the book and that have additionally been raised for them as researchers who are readers of the book
- Have been provided with strategies to improve their awareness of the researcher role and to better implement this awareness
- Have considered some of the tensions and challenges of greater awareness and implementation of the researcher role
- Have raised new considerations and questions about their own research and the research of others that will enable new critiques of their understanding of research and its uses.

Introduction

The following research activity, derived from the popular radio programme *Desert Island Discs*, may help researchers to think about their researcher-self – it requires them to consider the different aspects of themselves, how they understand and portray these and what they reveal about them as a whole.

RESEARCH ACTIVITY

The space-travelling researcher

Consider that you are about to have your memory wiped and to be left alone in space for a year. Before your rocket takes off you are allowed some last requests of 'items' to take with you to remind you of your Earth-bound self. These must include photographs, a book, words spoken by someone you know, some music, one memory from your childhood and one from your adulthood.

What would you choose?

Think carefully about what aspects of yourself you would want to be reminded of and how the items will do this. What do they say about you? Why do you want to be reminded of them?

In an unexpected twist, you are told on the day of take-off that there is a delay of 24 hours to the rocket flight. You are allowed to use this time to choose another set of the same items to be left with a person of your choosing on Earth. These will be returned to you when you come back.

Who would you choose to safeguard your identity this way? What items would you give them? Why do you want people to remember you this way? Why do you want these aspects of yourself to be what you return to after your experience?

This activity has been designed to provoke researchers to think carefully and in depth about who they are and how they wish to be perceived by others. By relating different aspects of the self to different artefacts (visual, literary, linguistic, audio and memory-based) researchers can understand the many forms of knowledge they have accessible to them about themselves and the different ways in which that knowledge can be disseminated to others. It will help to understand more of how they view themselves, their place and interaction in the world and their perception of how they acquire knowledge. It should also highlight what they consider most important about themselves and what this means to them.

Considering such questions in a research context, these researchers can gain more insight into what they wish to bring of themselves to research, how that shapes the focus and conduct of the research and what it means about their research interests.

An extension of the activity would be to consider it in relation to someone the researcher knows – who do you think they are? What makes them who they are? What are the different aspects of them that make them *them*? Having some insight into questions such as these about oneself and about others can help develop researcher knowledge and expertise.

(Re)considering the researcher role

> **Researcher View**
>
> 'I think the thing that underlies all of my research, I say this to students as well, is that I think I'm just innately nosey!'

Throughout the book there has been an emphasis on the researcher as a person who contributes and brings to the research aspects of themselves that are not always designed into the research practice. Researchers have been considered as neutral witnesses to research, co-constructors of the research, leaders of research projects, stakeholders in the research and implementers of the tasks required for research. Personal characteristics, motivations, agendas and interests of researchers and how they can play parts in the research have been discussed. The discussions and illustrations have shown that researchers can be aware of some of these and unaware of others. They have also shown that awareness can aid research, be used as an additional tool in research practice and present challenges to its management. Characteristics and drives that researcher are not aware of, such as the effect of personal circumstances and reasons for conducting the research, can impact on the research they carry out. The value of open communication, in personal reflexive dialogue and with other researchers, has been shown to bring insight and clarity to researchers as instruments and conductors of research practice. Ways in which the impact of these characteristics can change throughout the research process have been identified and strategies for learning to recognise and anticipate such changes outlined. Overall, key points in the book have constructed a picture of the researcher as someone who plays an important role in all research, in ways that can be made explicitly known to them and to the research audience, in ways that can be brought to their attention by others or through their own practice, and in ways that they may never be aware of.

Reflective Question: Think about some recent research that you have conducted. To what extent did you attend to your presence in the research? How did this attention influence decisions that you made in the conduct of the research and how much did this shape the final outcomes of the research?

Having awareness of the impact of the researcher on the research brings with it challenges of not only what to do with this awareness but also how to implement it into research practice. It raises questions about who you are as a researcher, why you are conducting research and what to do with this awareness in research practice. Researchers whose research approach calls for an objective, neutral and detached stance may struggle with implementing this awareness and with the demonstration of this awareness in the dissemination of their research. Researchers whose research approach calls for subjective awareness to be made clear, in practice and dissemination, may be challenged as to how much of this awareness to demonstrate and discuss in research reporting. These and other challenges can be discussed within the context of what they tell us of who the researcher is.

Researchers have many clearly identified tasks that span the range of the research process, from its original conception (and often several re-conceptions) to the dissemination of the final research reports. Such tasks will include identifying gaps in existing research literature, learning the theories about the idea, framing hypotheses or research questions to be tested and addressed in the research study, designing appropriate ways of investigating the ideas, obtaining ethical approval to conduct the research, identifying, accessing and recruiting appropriate participants, selecting the best methods of data collection and analysis, interpreting the results and findings reached, and displaying and disseminating the research study and its outcomes. To carry out the tasks, researchers may additionally have to recruit other researchers with expertise that they themselves do not have and consider financial, time and environmental constraints on the research.

The myriad tasks can be tackled in structured, systematic ways that bring about orderly progression through the research process but challenges to this can necessitate the tasks being reviewed, reordered or reconsidered in light of unforeseen influences. These may arise from unexpected findings in the research, difficulties and delays in gaining ethical approval or finding research participants. Events external to the research can mean that the researcher's time on the study is compromised if, for example, they become ill or are required to carry out professional tasks unrelated to the research. As the research unfolds, new findings, participants or interest can mean that new ways of investigating the topic may have to be developed or that new aspects of the topic come to the fore and demand investigation. With this comes new challenges and decisions about how to incorporate new questions or directions for the research and the relevance of these to the research hypothesis or question. Pluralistic and mixed-methods approaches explicitly allow for new avenues to be pursued in single research studies, often by an overt adherence to following the data that enables justification for new methods to be introduced to its interrogation. In other approaches, however, challenges can often be best addressed by refocusing the research or adding new studies to the project.

Researcher View

'I had always been interested how fathers who no longer lived with their children are discussed and presented in the media. To pursue this interest I decided to conduct research that analysed newspaper articles about this. As I began to gather articles for analysis I came across a few in which fathers talked about having been bereaved by the loss of their children's mother, and their ensuing difficulties in raising the children alone. This sometimes led to them having to commit the children to the care of others. Bereavement was an aspect of fathers' separation from their children that I had not thought about, and one that did not seem to have been extensively researched. I decided to change my research focus to fathers who had lost their children through bereavement of the children's mothers.'

In addition to methodological and topic-focused challenges to the researcher, the researcher's emotion and affect in the research process can have an impact. The chapters on positionality and the researcher as instrument included examples of researchers being influenced during and after data collection by the distressing nature of the topic, by feeling drawn to empathise with participants or being affected by similarities in experiences they were investigating because they resonated with experiences of their own. When considering the researcher as an instrument of the research, Chapter 3 discussed how life events and circumstances outside the research and their accompanying emotionality affected the ways in which the data was interpreted. Practical ways of addressing the influence of emotion that included preparing ways of presenting the researcher to participants and of debriefing participants after the research, developing sensitive and open communication in research dialogue with fellow researchers and taking care to debrief the researcher as well as the participants were identified.

The role of emotions in the researcher is one not often discussed in the context of conducting research. The lack of attention to this in the research literature can bring an inherent assumption that researcher emotion is not something that occurs in well-conducted research or if it does that it is something that should not be declared. When discussed in relation to subjectivity it is often done so in terms of undesirable emotions such as sadness. It may be regarded as a nuisance variable to be factored out of objective research. Recognising emotions, desirable or undesirable, in research, however, can provide an opportunity to improve research practice. By considering what it is about the research that may have evoked the emotion can help researchers to monitor their interactions with participants, pay attention to the construction of tests or questions to be put to participants and understand more of the role that researchers play in deciding how to interpret data.

Consider a researcher who finds themselves particularly happy about the results of a study. With awareness of this they may question whether it is because they were hoping to find results that supported or confirmed their own similar experiences or whether it was because they selected the right research design. A researcher who feels inexplicably sad during data collection can question whether this is because of meanings they are reading into data or whether it is because of outside events colouring their view. Researchers can also use their emotions to understand more about their experiences of research practice as the following words from a researcher describe.

Researcher View

'I am not sure whether this is an emotion or not but I do remember feeling very bored during an interview with a police officer about their expectations of promotion. As they reeled off lists of the duties that would be required of them if they gained promotion I felt sleepy and disconnected. At the time I put this down to the fact that the interview was being conducted in the evening following a long day at work. In the weeks following the interview I came to realise that I was putting off analysing it. Initially thinking this was because I still harboured my experience of it as being boring, discussion with colleagues about this meant that I began to understand that many of the duties that he was describing were similar to those I find least rewarding and boring about my own job. Although I am not a police officer, much of my work involves administration and I really don't enjoy this, not finding it stimulating and often resenting its intrusion into the much more enjoyable face-to-face interactions that form part of my professional role. Once I understood this as an explanation of my boredom during the interview I was able to understand the accompanying irritation I felt during it as being my own irritation at those aspects of my job that I find boring. So yes, I suppose that is an example of how awareness of my emotions, albeit provoked by an awareness of my experience as a whole, helped improve my research practice.'

A challenging aspect of emotionality, arguably in all walks of life, is the difficulty in recognising it. It is sometimes easier not to identify unacceptable emotions (perhaps ones that evoke feelings of pleasure at the misfortune of others) and sometimes difficult to name feelings, instead just knowing that 'something is not as it should be'. For the researcher this can be disorientating and raise new concerns about not being professional in their research conduct. It would seem more conducive to the quality of the research to recognise the presence of emotionality in the choice, conduct and interpretation of research, and so to harness it to the good of the research. Such harnessing may mean recognising an emotional investment in the research and developing strategies to ensure that this does not bias it or it may mean finding ways of displacing the emotions from the research design.

Researchers can do this in a number of ways: drawing on the support of others, recognising their own strengths and limitations in research conduct and being open to those of other researchers, maintaining confidential reflective journals to acknowledge and query emotions in the research experience and using supervision and research mentorship to highlight the presence and impact of emotions on research conduct, to suggest a few. It can also be valuable to the researcher and to the research practice to consider whether the emotions are arising from the research or from outside experience being brought to the research.

Research team members and leaders can take responsibility for enabling the team to recognise and discuss the role of emotions in the research being conducted. They can develop platforms for safe discussion of emotions to enable the research to be designed and conducted accordingly. Researchers can be apprised of clear strategies of what they should do in research situations that provoke concern about participants or distress to the researchers. This in itself can help researchers to recognise and manage emotions effectively, with reduced distress to themselves. The threat of not having this clarity in place, and the confusion that can arise, is described below by a researcher:

Researcher View

'Well there were always issues about sensitivity that arose because I did this for years in different sort of capacities. Originally as a research assistant and eventually heading the programme. And different things would occur at different times really. But one of them that comes to mind is, one is somebody who was threatening to commit suicide, and I know it sounds strange now, but our ethics at the time were that we couldn't intervene in anyway because we were actually an academic department. It wasn't our brief, we couldn't cross boundaries with medics or clinicians. So for somebody as, you know, you couldn't do anything for them. But we were quite clear that we had to and after a long debate about telling the GP, the GP was just not interested and said "she'll never do it". But you know going over the boundary for us was to report on it when we weren't really supposed to in our ethics and er, um, the Head of our Department, um, actually came up with a thing, "well as head of this research programme with the ethics we've got, I can't advocate that you would do this, but in your own capacity as an individual I really think you should" and that was the way it was formulated.'

Researching across differences

A recurring theme that has threaded through this book has been that of challenges and benefits of researching with difference. For the single researcher these differences may revolve around being an outsider researcher who is investigating issues within communities they are not part of. Recognised differences in experience, language, knowledge and assumptions can contribute to the outsider researcher role by prompting researchers to seek more detail in the data in the quest to be informed of issues they know little about. Such differences can also challenge the researcher to be aware of overlooking or misinterpreting nuances in the provision of information to them. Researchers conducting research as team members can encounter differences in research agendas, purposes and status between academic and professional roles. These differences have to be navigated by clear communication and strategies that allow for querying and review of research issues throughout the process. Interpersonal differences can occur for researchers working alone or as part of a team, in the research conduct with other researchers and with participants, and in the dissemination of the research at events for different research audiences.

Also common to all researchers are differences in paradigmatic approaches. The training that researchers receive in conducting research typically focuses on the dominant method of the discipline. Whilst in many social sciences the methods include both qualitative and quantitative methods, in many other disciplines traditional scientific objective methods are prioritised. This means that many researchers at the outset of their research careers are knowledgeable only of positivistic research paradigms and quantitatively based research methods. These approaches are associated with the researcher role being one of neutrality and detachment, although this book has highlighted arguments for these purely objective stances to be challenged by considering the subjectivity of choices about topics to investigate, framing of research designs, choices of tests for the data, interpretation of results and reporting of the research.

Despite the common mono-method training approach to research, however, many researchers do bring methods from different paradigms to their research. More complex research questions are able to be addressed using both qualitative and quantitative methods. Series of studies can be designed so that the results of one inform the development of another or results and findings from studies conducted concurrently can be integrated to answer research queries more comprehensively. Working across paradigms brings particular challenges to researchers because each have different epistemological underpinnings that require researchers to carefully consider their view of the constitution of knowledge and how it is accessed. If they hold to only one view the research methods available to them are constrained. Seeking to apply and combine different views of knowledge and its acquisition can present difficult challenges to researchers and many debates about the epistemological incoherence abound in research literature. They range from a position that differing epistemologies cannot be commensurate to one where the best tools (methods) for the job are brought to the research and epistemological concerns overlooked in order to reach useful outcomes.

Mixed-methods and pluralistic researchers

The benefits of combining paradigms in research have been seen in mixed-methods and qualitative pluralistic research. Mixed-methods research allows for triangulation, the use of human stories of experience to enrich studies and the development of wider generalisable studies from small-scale in-depth qualitative studies. Pluralistic qualitative research seeks complexities of human experience to be better understood by examining the same phenomenon from many perspectives. Ontological pluralism assumes that the world, and the ways that sense is made of it, is multiple. Different philosophical positions are regarded as mutually informing rather than mutually exclusive and this allows researchers to hold tensions lightly together and interact with multiple paradigms simultaneously. In contrast, epistemological pluralism uses multiple analytic methods that are underpinned by a consistent ontological position to produce diverse, yet complementary, forms of knowledge and removes the difficulty of epistemological incoherence for researchers. This reflects the belief that multiple forms of knowledge can be produced without imposing concomitant ontological claims (Clarke, Caddick, & Frost, in press). Both approaches aim to draw on the strengths and value of each method employed in pursuit of the best possible ways of addressing the research query.

The pluralistic researcher combines analytical tools from different paradigms to address bias in assumptions about the nature of reality. In recognition that the kind of knowledge being sought influences the type of research questions that can be asked and informs how data is interrogated, these researchers seek a holistic view by considering it within many dimensions. Different paradigmatic approaches can seek to access different dimensions that make up experiences by considering reactions, beliefs, thoughts, feelings and actions, using a range of methods. Approaches can be considered on a continuum that ranges from the experiential to the discursive and from the empiricist to the theoretical.

By regarding people's experiences as multi-dimensional, pluralistic researchers can seek out multi-ontological understandings of the world that are held by individuals (Mark & Snowden, 2006). Frameworks of ontological and epistemological multiplicity and multi-dimensionality can be both appropriate and helpful in understanding such realities and enable researchers to move from 'either/or' positions of exploration to 'both/and' positions of inquiry. For pluralistic researchers, this stance is not in pursuit of a definitive truth about experience but more to gain further understanding of the complexities and nuances of human life (Frost et al., 2010).

This reasoning is one that has been adopted in the counselling field by Mick Cooper and John McLeod (2011). In a recent book these researchers/counsellors set out the aim of bringing together a set of principles and meta-strategies of counselling and psycho-therapy that are rooted in ethical principles, to better recognise and serve the changing needs of clients. The pluralistic approach priori-tises collaborative working between therapist and client. Based on the principles that multiple change processes exist and that decisions about which change process to follow are achieved in consultation with the clients, this approach seeks to be employable by therapists from a range of backgrounds, whilst also recognising the clients as self-therapists.

The concept of pluralism in counselling and psychotherapy rep-resents a form of theoretical integration that is held together by philosophical and ethical valuing of diversity. The pluralistic therapist strives to help their client to select from all the possibilities in order to address their specific problem. Clients are viewed as active agents who are engaged in using whatever tools and resources are available to them in order to construct a more satisfying life.

Both researchers and therapists adopting pluralist approaches place the focus of their practice on the data or the client rather than on the method or technique. Both see the data or the client as holding mean-ings and understandings that can be accessed and revealed through interactive engagement with the researcher or therapist.

Bringing a pluralistic approach to understanding social interac-tion and human experience in qualitative research allows for flex-ibility in the search for meaning in the data by viewing accounts from many perspectives. The choice of perspectives brought to the data is informed by the data, in combination with the researchers' knowledge, hunches and epistemological stance in relation to the research topic. Layers of meaning that are of relevance to the research question can be extracted or combined to give a more holistic insight that better reflects the complexity of the phenomenon and its descrip-tion. This has been found to be particularly useful when researching topics with no ontological consensus such as anomalous experience (Steffen & Coyle, 2010), where the researcher has insider status, such as mothers researching mothers (Frost, 2006) and where services are being developed for people who contest meanings ascribed to particu-lar behaviours (e.g. Warner & Spandler, 2011).

Bringing a pluralistic approach to counselling is achieved by developing a relationship between client and therapist that allows the range of ideas and practices available to be selected to best match the needs of the client. Through dialogue and interaction shared understandings of the client's problems are reached, goals regarding therapy are set, tasks for achieving the goals identified and methods of fulfilling the tasks devised. All are regularly reviewed in interactive conversation and reflection. The same approach can be used by researchers who can regard the research problem as the 'client' and the methods and paradigms brought to its exploration as the 'techniques'. Dialogue between the two is an interactive reflexive stance that enables ongoing review of goals and the ways in which they are worked towards.

Underlying any pluralistic approach is a tension. The desire to be open and inclusive to practice and methods is pitted against the need to avoid an 'anything goes' approach that threatens the rigour of the research for researchers. For pluralistic researchers, questions can be asked about how they assess 'depth' of insight and how this differs to that obtained using one method. There is also a tension for pluralistic researchers in recognising but not being able to reach an ideal outcome of understanding that accords with affording choice and inclusivity. In reality, though, this may not be achievable – finding researchers or therapists who offer the methods or techniques being sought may not be possible and compromise may be necessary.

Being an ethical researcher

Being ethical means distinguishing between right and wrong in behaviour. Being an ethical researcher means, at the very least, applying professional codes of conduct to the way in which the research is carried out. Chapter 1 highlighted that in addition to adhering to required ethical behaviours, researchers can consider bringing a positive ethical stance to their research. A positive ethical stance considers the added value and benefits of research to those who take part in it and to those for whom its implications may be relevant.

Most professional practices and academic disciplines have codes of conduct, one of the best known perhaps being that of the medical profession: the Hippocratic oath ('first of all, do no harm'). Most codes of conduct provide a list of required actions and guidelines to help researchers take decisions that will maintain professionalism and ensure the safety and protection of research participants.

Illustrative guidelines for the conduct of ethical research

Ensure potential participants have sufficient information to provide informed consent to take part in the research	This means developing information sheets that succinctly summarise the research study, the reasons why it is to be carried out, what participants will be asked to do, how the data will be analysed and to whom it will be disseminated.
Ensure anonymity of participants	This means ensuring that demographic, socio-economic and personal details about participants do not enable them to be recognised in the final research write-up. As well as changing or obscuring such details about individuals or groups, this means anonymising names of geographical location and home or work settings.
Ensure confidentiality of data	This means sharing the data only with agreed others who are usually also committed to the research study. This can be research supervisors and mentors as well as research team members. Data should be stored in ways that protect it being accessed by others. Physical data should be kept in secure, locked containers. Data stored electronically should be password-protected.
Demonstrate the value of the research study	This means that research should be conducted because there is an identified need for it. This may be because a gap in knowledge in existing research literature or a gap in professional practice has been found through a process of systematic critique and evaluation.
Do not falsify data	This means making clear that the data used in the research is original (or stated as secondary data in research that re-analyses existing data), gathered by the researcher for the purposes of the study and not falsified for any reason (for example, to provide 'better' results).
Acknowledge the work or contribution of others in the research study	This means making clear all those involved in the research. In addition to other researchers, this may mean stakeholders such as those based in the community in which the research is conducted, service providers or government and policy-making representatives, all of whom may have helped to shape the research study.

Many sets of guidelines go beyond these basic requirements to expect potential participants to be debriefed after taking part in the research, researchers to have been validated by both their research institutions and the places where they are planning to conduct the research (which may require additional checks for criminal convictions or for working with children) and participants to have opportunities to see and comment on the data they have provided and the interpretations and tests performed on it.

It can be seen that decisions about how to implement ethical guidelines lie primarily in the hands of the researcher conducting the research, once again centring them within the research. Although laid out clearly by most professions and disciplines, the implementation of such guidelines in practice can present challenges to researchers.

Providing sufficient information to participants so that they know what is expected of them and what will happen to the data they provide may mean going beyond simply giving them a summary of the study. Researchers have to consider how the information is presented and to whom. Language used should be meaningful to participants, using other forms of presentation than language such as pictures and sound if necessary. There may be a need to provide the information more than once and in more than one form for some participants. Parents and carers may need to be aware of the study. Employers or others in positions of authority may need (or want) to know what is being researched, how and what will be done with the outcomes. Potential participants should have opportunities to seek further information from the researcher before giving consent and they should have details of people other than the researcher, such as the research leader or supervisor, who they can contact with concerns or queries about the research.

Maintaining anonymity of participants may be difficult if the research is conducted in a small clearly defined community such as a business organisation. Although data may be anonymised during the conduct of the research, when it is written up the setting in which it was conducted may be, or may need to be, clearly identifiable and therefore the people within it may be recognisable, too. Extra care should be taken to anonymise these details and to consider where the research is disseminated.

Ensuring the safe storage of data can be compromised if the researcher is working within an organisation that does not have provision for them to store data there. Researcher's homes may be busy and pose threats from curious children poking into cupboards or studies. Storage of data on computers may mean using cloud storage to which members of the public may be able to gain access. Questions about the confidentiality of 'big data', large data sets gathered about individuals from their interaction with public services, raise issues of breaches of security and privacy.

To help researchers make decisions in ethically responsible ways, there are a number of principles they can bring to their research conduct. The British Psychological Society suggests four domains of responsibility in which statements of values based on fundamental beliefs can guide 'ethical reasoning, decision-making and behaviour' (British Psychological Society, 2009, p. 9) which are summarised below.

Summary of ethical principles for ethical decision-making

(British Psychological Society, 2009)

Respect: valuing dignity and worth in others, with sensitivity to dynamics of authority or influence and with particular regard to the rights of others, including those of privacy and self.

Competence: valuing the continuing development and maintenance of high standards of competence by recognising limits and threats to knowledge, skill, training, education and experience.

Responsibility: valuing responsibilities to others and to the profession, including the avoidance of harm, prevention of misuse and abuse of their contributions to society.

Integrity: valuing honesty, accuracy, clarity and fairness in interactions with others and in all facets of professional endeavours.

Overlying all the guidelines, values and principles of ethical practice is the researcher's role in bringing new insight and meaning to data provided by participants. With this comes responsibility for recognising not only that these may be meanings that participants do not agree with but also that these may be meanings that participants are not aware of. Researchers, similar to psychotherapists, are often seeking meanings in data provided by other people. In contrast to psychotherapeutic work, however, researchers rarely do this in the presence of the participants. Data is collected and taken away for study, analysis and interpretation. The time between collecting the data and analysing it may extend into weeks or months, as opposed to psychotherapeutic practice in which interpretations are made in the presence of the client and usually immediately offered back to them for their consideration. Research data interpretation does not always involve the participant and is rarely carried out at the time of its collection.

Interpretations may be made using statistical and other tests or may be brought by studying language, visual data, and context. In both situations, the researcher usually works with the data in the absence of the person who has provided it. Subjective researchers will recognise their role in interpreting data, seeking to identify and make clear the knowledge, theories, assumptions and methods they have brought to it. Objective researchers may regard themselves as simply applying tests to confirm or disconfirm theories and hypotheses. However, as this book has sought to illustrate, the fact that the researcher makes decisions about what to do with information provided by other people inextricably links them with the data and necessitates recognition of the possibility for abuse of this power.

To address this, ethical researchers can consider not only what they are doing with the data but also why they have chosen this form of its interpretation. They can ask questions of themselves about the value to the participant of their data being used this way and the value to a wider community of it having been done. Ethical researchers can also consider how they present the results and findings of their research and to whom. Are they going to provide those who took part in the research with reports of the research? Are they going to offer opportunities for them to comment on the way the research has been conducted? If participants do provide this feedback, what are researchers going to do with it? At what point will they cease seeking input and incorporating feedback?

Ethical researchers can also consider what constitutes data in studies. What about those interesting accounts or references to experiences that are spoken about after the interview has ended? What about data that does not fit with the rest of the data set?

Potentially, the questions are endless and individual researchers striving to be ethical in their research practice will need to consider carefully the limits of their research practice and the individual studies they conduct. Limits may be imposed by the institution in which they are conducting the research: time, money and co-operation from others. Limits may also lie in the reasons for doing the research. If the study is an initial scoping study developed to inform a second larger primary study, researchers may consider initial data collected as more, or less, important, for example.

The following researcher view describes the range and uses of considerations of interpretations:

Researcher View

'And I haven't I suppose ever really done research where I'm the subject, but I've written quite a few things where in various different ways I've used my subjectivity or my experiences… So I wrote a paper, it was for a conference, initially I wrote it for a conference on belonging in a city. And it was really about an encounter that I had in a park. I was walking my dog in a park on a cold Saturday afternoon and came across a woman who was lying kind of on the ground under a tree in the leaves. And it's a discussion of the discussion that we had, the encounter that we had. So it's not really about me and my subjectivity, but it's absolutely about my experiencing this very particular encounter that developed between me and someone else and then the kind of thing that I'm doing with the paper I suppose is making some broader reflections about what belonging means in a neo-liberal society and in the context of welfare state cuts and so on. Why is this woman lying on the ground sort of talking about killing herself? So using the kind of self as a tool, recognising that intersubjectivity is absolutely always crucial. We may or may not focus on it. So I've also done plenty of interviews where I don't go down that road, where I'm taking them more on a straightforward basis of what the interviewee said to me.'

Another researcher describes the importance of dissemination in respecting the contributions made by participants:

Researcher View

'I imagine that the people who were interviewed also remember it because they wouldn't normally do that and many people say they have never spoken about their childhood, so it was kind of privileged information if you like. And they would go on for hours and often on several visits. So you are talking about a lot of contact really. I think a good interview was a very intimate experience sort of sharing minds really. So you do have to be prepared on both sides. Um, but I wouldn't have done research differently, you know it was the only thing that was really important was getting these stories. And this is why I think the dissemination is important and there's a lot of discussion now whether you can make any of these a bit more public, or at least more available to other researchers and what's the ethics of that and what's the copyright and all the rest of it. My feeling is that the stories were valuable and people would want to know that something useful had been done with them. Obviously they can't be public and recognisable but still chucking them away I think would be insulting. [Laughs]. Yes.'

Perhaps the best way to conclude this discussion of what being an ethical researcher can really mean is to suggest that researchers go beyond the guidelines laid down for their professions and disciplines to think about what the research really means to them and to others taking part in it. By doing this, ethical researchers can consider the required and anticipated research practice but also the values, beliefs and morals that they practice in everyday life and which they can bring to the research that they conduct.

Reflective Question: What do you consider to be unethical behaviour in everyday life? How do the principles of respect and integrity inform your considerations? Think about issues of politics or education – is it ever right for the rights of the few to be overridden for the greater good of the many?

The researcher and research quality

The inherent assumption throughout this book has been that researchers wishing to raise awareness of their role and its impact on research are doing so in order to enhance the quality of research. Each chapter in the book has considered the researcher from different perspectives and within the context of knowing more of what they bring to research, how they bring it and why it matters to the research. In formal research terms there are measures and expectations about the quality of research and how it can be evaluated. In positivistic experimental and quasi-experimental research approaches, demonstrations of objectivity, validity, reliability, generalisability and robustness are expected. In interpretivist research approaches, transparency, reflexivity, rigour, coherence and contribution to the area are regarded as important markers of sound high-quality research, although they are not the only ones (Frost & Kinmond, 2012).

This book has emphasised throughout the status of objectivity and subjectivity in all research approaches and highlighted the value of reflexivity for considering the researcher role. In addition to this general evaluation tool, different research paradigms incorporate different mechanisms for evaluating research and many debates centre on questions of the transferability between them.

Broadly speaking, positivistic research evaluation considers the variables, the control mechanisms and the appropriateness of the methods used to test the hypothesis. Interpretivist research approaches consider the trustworthiness of the research by critiquing the descriptions of how and from whom the data was collected, what methods were employed and how in their analysis and what of the research is presented in the final write-up, all within the specific context of the research study to allow for the inclusion of subjectivity.

Both approaches to evaluation bring challenges for the researcher. The objective researcher is challenged over whether, where and how to incorporate subjectively informed decisions made in the research process. The subjective researcher is challenged to show flexibility that accommodates the fluidity of the research whilst avoiding a checklist approach or an 'anything goes' presentation.

The positivist researcher who seeks to include the influence they have brought to the research is likely to risk, at best, this inclusion being dismissed and, at worst, having all the research labelled as invalid. One way to circumnavigate these threats may be for the objective researcher to make very clear at what points in the research they brought subjective considerations and at what points these decisions influenced the research direction or outcome. This need not interfere in the presentation with the reporting of how the data were tested nor with the reporting of results. Instead the inclusion of insightful awareness of their influence on the choices of tests and measures brought to the research may add positively to the critique of the research. For example, demonstration that the researcher has considered language and focus of survey questions to allow for gender differences will show readers of the research that the data collected can be reliable in this respect. Highlighting, as the summary of research by Ryan and Golden (2006) in Chapter 2 did, that at unexpected moments additional data were gathered, will show readers that the participants were engaged with the research and perhaps therefore that responder bias was reduced.

Subjective researchers face a different set of challenges. The expectation is that it is in the demonstration of their awareness of what they bring to the research and how their relationship with it influences and shapes it provides a measure of its quality. Yet studies have shown that researchers can be concerned that including too much of this information can take away from the research focus, particularly where differences in consensual and individual analyses by researchers are numerous, as the summary of the King et al. (2008) study in Chapter 4 demonstrated. Gough (2003) points out that subjective researchers can also be at risk of being too reflexive and falling into the realms of narcissism, similarly taking the research focus away from the topic and on to the researcher.

One way in which subjective researchers can address these concerns is by maintaining field diaries and reflective journals. The field diaries can function primarily as catalogues of what was done in the research process. The reflective journals can focus on the experiences of doing the research. Ongoing and final review of both will aid recall and clarity for the researcher of the key decisions made in the research process. It will equip them to evaluate the resultant actions within the research and provide them with the basis for relevant synthesis of the two, to present to readers.

For all researchers, the way in which they enhance the quality of the research is through an adherence to the research question or hypothesis. By keeping this firmly in mind, researchers can consider every aspect of the research process with regard to how it is best suited to the research focus. If they add to the considerations of research design, methods and data interpretation, considerations of what role they have played in these, the final reporting of the research can incorporate all these elements, implicitly in places and explicitly in other places. The craft of writing this up is another layer in this process, to which the next section turns.

Reflective Question: What are the key points in the research process at which the researcher may have the most influence? Think about the tasks of research conduct: identifying the research question or hypothesis, designing the research study, eliciting and gathering data, analysing and testing data, reporting results and findings.

The researcher and reporting research

A key aspect of the research process is disseminating the research after it has been carried out. As the book has shown, one of the aims of the research dissemination is to provide consumers and readers of the research with enough information for them to form their own critique of it and make decisions about its use for their own research or practice. To do this, many academic researchers choose (and are encouraged by their institutions) to publish in academic journals, the primary sources of research literature. However, many challenges to journal publication exist for researchers, including selecting and writing for the journals most likely to be read by the desired research audience and having manuscripts accepted for publication. Although it varies across disciplines and journals, it is not unusual for journal manuscript rejection rates to be upwards of 50 per cent. In addition to this, difficulties in finding reviewers for submitted journal manuscripts and the publication process itself means that researchers can be waiting for months and even years before they see their research published. With this comes concerns that the research has been carried out (and published) elsewhere or that new knowledge about the research topic comes to light, making the first report outdated. If a paper submitted for publication is ultimately rejected following the review process (typically comprising reviews by two or three peer reviewers) the research has to be submitted to another journal and the process started all over again. Most journals require that articles submitted for potential publication to them are not simultaneously submitted to other journals.

In a commissioned review of the dissemination process (Hughes et al., 2000) the Joseph Rowntree Foundation found that the time and money needed for the dissemination process are often under-considered in the research planning and funding provision. Researchers and funders do not factor in what is needed to write up the research for audiences other than the funders, for whom a report of the project, and how their money has been spent, is usually a requirement of granting the research. This can mean that once the research has been completed and the report for funders written, the research team can break up and its members move on to other tasks (or simply relish the extra time they have available once the research is complete). To bring the team back together for the purposes of further dissemination can be difficult, particularly when the role of the research has different priorities for different team members. Most academic researchers plan to publish in journals as part of the research process but practitioner researchers may not consider this as important as implementing the results of the research in professional practice.

Researcher View

'We did then have a bit of a gap when the actual funded period of the research had finished and all the data had been collected, and now we are sort of coming back to it, to try and get the stuff written up and published, which … So the challenges were trying to keep up that communication and then like I said once the funded project ended, the communication sort of fell away a bit because for them it was, then they had written their report for the funding and that was it. But obviously for us one of our objectives was to get this stuff published in the public domain. So I have just, before Christmas actually, just reconnected with the group and we are meeting in a couple of weeks to come back and look at the data again and make sure that we can actually get a good publication out of it.'

In writing up research, challenges for researchers also lie in how to present the research. Different journals have different audiences and articles are tailored to the interests of these audiences. For the researcher, this means selecting aspects of the research to convey in the article. This can mean having to leave out aspects that they feel might add more depth or insight to it or aspects they are more interested in. For example, some researchers may be less interested in writing for methodologically focused journals than for topic-focused journals yet may have used an innovative methodology in the research study that they think can be of benefit in other arenas and the details of which should be made known in a substantial article. Keeping in mind that the research write-up has to be effective in making the research known more widely and accessible to audiences who may not be familiar with the topic or the language used to describe the research, researchers have to find engaging ways to attract and retain audiences.

Researcher subjectivity, which has been a key theme of this book, presents particular challenges for researchers writing up for dissemination. Chenail (1995) advocates 'openness' in research writing. This is a mixture of reflexivity, description and detail and this requires the author/researcher to present as much detail as possible (within constraints of word limits and presentation style) of the research and the way it was carried out. This can be achieved by adopting a 'two-study approach' (Chenail, 1995) in which the author/researcher considers both the research project and their study of that study.

This approach creates space to acknowledge the development of the method and its application throughout the study and the impact of the researcher on its use. The resultant write-up includes details of the decisions the researcher made and how and why they were reached. The researcher has several opportunities to examine the particulars of the steps taken during the study, from the formation of the research question and the selection of data elicitation settings and processes to the analysis of the data collected and presentation of the findings.

Chenail argues that this 'spirit of openness' (Chenail, 1995, p. 2) can be achieved by considering the 'other' in the process at all times. The other may be the intended audience for the write-up, the participants who took part in the study and colleagues and peers who comment and read the work. By communicating details and descriptions of the process of the study openly to the other, the spirit of openness engenders one of trust and of the research being considered trustworthy and rigorously conducted. The additional challenge for the researcher may be to find a journal that is open to accepting this style of research write-up, although there are an increasing number now emerging, albeit primarily in the qualitative research domain (for example, *Qualitative Research* and *Qualitative Psychology*).

Research dissemination is not confined to publications in academic journals and arguably, to be of greater use, researchers should look to disseminate their work beyond those realms accessed most commonly only by other researchers. Researchers can consider all the stakeholders in the research and consider how best to share the research with them. Stakeholders may be community members who will benefit much more from hearing about the research outcomes in accessible language presented to them in non-academic environments than from reference to an academic journal, often only available through university library subscription. Researchers often write short research summaries in plain English. Indeed, it is often a requirement of funders that such reports are written both to publicise the research before it is carried out and to summarise it at its conclusion, for distribution to community members. Community-based events can be held away from the research institution if appropriate, to which community members are invited to come and hear about the research and raise questions they may have about it. Costs and time for such events should be factored into financial considerations and include venue hire, publicity costs, refreshments, security, audio/video equipment and travel expenses for community members. In addition to community members, stakeholders may include service providers, service users and policy-makers. These audiences are likely to be interested in particular aspects of the research and also more familiar with the language associated with the research focus. Researchers can extract the policy and practice-related implications of research for these audiences and disseminate them in written and spoken form at smaller-scale events, perhaps at the service providers and policy-makers' offices or at the places where services are delivered, to reduce their travel time and costs.

The media provides another avenue for dissemination that researchers can consider. Local newspapers and radio stations may be interested to hear about research affecting the local community or in which the local community have participated. Issues of national concern may be picked up on by media representatives attending conferences where researchers are presenting research. Many of the bodies that regulate research amongst academic disciplines offer media training to enable researchers prepare for engagement with the media and to effectively use it for dissemination of their research.

The rise of electronic networks and blogs through platforms such as WordPress (see, for example, www.npqr.wordpress.com), Twitter and Facebook provides researchers with myriad ways of disseminating their work to a worldwide audience. In addition to publicising research that is planned or being carried out, electronic media allows for researchers' personal insight to be aired, where perhaps they cannot be accommodated within the formality of research journals.

Webinars and other online seminars and courses allow researchers to deliver or take part in live events in which their research may be of interest to others.

Conclusions

This book set out in its Preface its aims to consider the researcher, and their impact on the research they conduct, on the premise that the researcher plays a key role in all aspects of research.

The book has striven to do this by discussing theoretical and empirical evidence for this, by seeking to draw these together with research examples and views from researchers themselves, by considering different aspects and circumstances that researchers find themselves in and by posing questions to the readers of the book. In some ways it is hoped that the book has answered some questions but in doing so raised others.

The book has sought to blur the boundaries between different approaches to formal research whilst at the same time acknowledge some of the challenges particular to different paradigms. In doing so, there have been practical, epistemological and personal issues that have had to be considered in detail.

Overall, however, the book can perhaps conclude that 'the researcher' is far more than the person who carried out a series of tasks to conduct research. Whilst it is obviously important for researchers, and those who use research, to know what these tasks are and how to achieve them effectively, the discussions, illustrations and personal views have highlighted that the researcher as a person is a key influence on the research. The ways in which personal characteristics, action, thoughts and feelings intersect with the practical requirements of research have shown not only that the tasks are not distinct from these but also the value that consideration of them can bring to the quality of the research. But these considerations are not as simple to address as the tasks that need to be done. Although the ways in which the researcher intersects with the tasks can be anticipated and prepared for in some ways, the book has also shown that in other ways it is the lack of knowledge about oneself as a researcher, how the researcher is perceived by others involved in the research and the impact they have on the research that can influence it the most, for better or worse. A passionate engagement with the research may mean that inherently the researcher sets out to consider all the concerns that may influence the research. A commitment to research a topic in order to bring about transformative change may mean that a researcher takes extra care to find representative participants for the research. Similarly, conducting research amongst a busy schedule of professional practice or other duties may mean that a researcher does not have sufficient energy or time to devote to the research, resulting in oversights and the obscuring of key aspects of it. Researchers' views in the book have shown the place and value of retrospective reflection on the research they have conducted, to highlight the role they have played and consider why the research took the direction that it did.

In conclusion then perhaps all that can be said is that 'the researcher' is a different person and has a different impact on research at different points in its conduct. Rather than seeking to define and delineate this impact in ways similar to defining and delineating the tasks that need to be carried out to do the research, the researcher can have awareness of their impact and find ways to address this before, during and after the research they conduct. In this way, they are likely not only to improve the research they do but to gain more personal satisfaction and fulfilment from it. In a final researcher view, perhaps researchers can best be summed up as people who are simply interested in other people:

Researcher View

'I just like to hear about other people's lives and I think I've managed to do that through my research. So that sort of, intrigue I suppose would be a better way of expressing it in professional terms.'

Closing reflection from author/researcher

This book started with a reflection from me on what I hoped to achieve in writing it and how I was anticipating setting about doing that. In this closing reflection, written after I have finished the writing of the book, I find myself considering the book as a research project of its own:

This book has discussed, illustrated and debated the inclusion of subjectivity in its consideration of the researcher in the research process. As I have drawn on my own experiences, researched the evidence, interviewed others and considered theories about this I have had an increasing awareness of my own subjective involvement in how the book has been written In many ways similar to research, the writing of the book has involved identifying a gap in the existing literature

(Continued)

available to researchers, considering how to frame an inquiry into this gap, devising a plan for addressing that gap (which not only involved discussing it with publishers but also considering how to structure it in a way useful to researchers) and embarking on the process of writing it. The final write-up is evident; its value and usefulness will be determined in due course by its audience.

Throughout the project I have held the awareness that my interest in this topic has arisen from my experiences of conducting research, of teaching others to conduct research and of accessing the research conducted by others. The knowledge I have gained through these processes and the questions that have been raised for me by them have been what has driven my commitment to the project. At the same time, I have been aware that my knowledge, assumptions and understandings have been biased by my own research practice and interests that have lain primarily in qualitative and applied research. As an author striving to develop writing that is accessible and of interest to researchers using all forms of research (and my personal conviction that research should not be divided between different paradigms but should be approached in the most appropriate way to inquire into the research topic). I have had to educate myself about research approaches and topics that I did not previously know and learn from people who I would not usually encounter in my everyday practice of research. This has been at times enlightening and insightful but if I am honest (as I would advocate reflection to be!) at other times I have found myself to be challenged by aspects of this, sometimes because of my emotional responses to the research topic and at other times in understanding why and how a particular methodology was employed.

Realising and acknowledging this enabled me to understand more of myself as a researcher, my research interests and how I impact on the research that I do. The outcome I hope is a book that recognises subjectivity throughout but does not impose mine overly on the information that is presented.

Glossary

Cartesian dualism: a term arising from Descartes's claim that minds and bodies are distinct from each other but causally related: the mind receives signals from the body; the body responds to plans made in the mind.

Comprehensive triangulation: in Flick's (2010) terms the combining of researcher triangulation, theory triangulation and methodological triangulation to provide access to data on different levels and with different qualities and provide a credible integration of theories, methodologies and subjectivities that have been brought to a study.

Confounding variable: a variable in statistical models that correlates with both the dependent and the independent variables.

Constructivism: an ontology that holds that reality is generated by individuals and groups (as opposed to positivism, which holds that reality is fixed and external).

Control variables: a variable that tests the relative impact of independent variables by being held fixed and unchanging.

Critical friends: similar to mentoring and coaching, the role of a critical friend is to provocatively question and supportively critique another's work in order to enhance their professional practice.

Critical realism: describes the interface between natural and social worlds to question assumptions and origins of knowledge.

Dependent variable: a variable that is measured in studies to see how changes in the independent variable cause changes in it.

Empathic interpretation: the process of seeking meaning in data that is about experience by exploring only what is presented. The focus is on the material itself and not on what may lie behind it.

Epistemology: considers the nature and origin of knowledge, identifying how the knowledge is reached and what its limits are.

Experimenter bias: overt or implicit influence by the researcher that affects the study results.

Feminist research: an umbrella term for research that explores how practices, knowledge, assumptions and social structures affect women.

Generalisable: results from studies that determine the reproducibility of measurements within a sample population to a wider population.

Independent variable: a variable that is not based on other variables, remains fixed and is not influenced or altered by changes in other variables.

Interpretivism: assumes that reality is accessed through social constructions such as language and therefore also centres the researcher within the study.

Investigator triangulation: the consideration of different subjectivities and concepts brought to a study by different researchers.

Methodological triangulation: the consideration of different methods and approaches brought to a study.

Methodology: the paradigmatic approach (usually qualitative, quantitative or mixed) brought to a study.

Ontology: beliefs and assumptions held by individuals about what exists and what is real in the world.

Paradigms: frameworks of theories and methods with which research is conducted.

Participant demand characteristics: cues that participants perceive as the expectations of the researcher of how they should behave or respond. Responding to the cues means that the outcome of the research can be altered by adjustments made by participants in their behaviour.

Positive ethics: the benefits brought to research topics and participants by the research being carried out.

Positivism: an ontology that holds that an external, universal and fixed reality exists and can be identified and described.

Post positivism: an amendment to positivism which contends that the influence of the researcher informs what is identified and how it is described.

Pragmatic research: a form of inquiry that includes human imagination, interpretation, intentions and values by drawing on a mixture of methods considered most appropriate to achieve richness and depth in the research experience. Research outcomes are tested in external reality with the aim of producing knowledge that is socially useful.

Qualitative research: an approach to research that seeks out meanings and descriptions of actions, beliefs, experiences and events to understand more of how people make sense of themselves and the world around them. It considers context and interaction usually through exploration of non-numerical data such as language, visual images and observed behaviours.

Quantitative research: an approach to research that seeks out information about the world that can be understood using numbers. It uses statistical tests and examines cause and effect relationships to confirm or disconfirm hypotheses.

Realism: the ontological view that reality exists that is external to the mind. Realist researchers aim to identify objects, systems, cognitions, and so on, as well as abstract concepts such as beliefs and perceptions.

Reflexivity: a quality criteria that calls for researchers to reflect on their role, input and influence on the research process by requiring them to raise their awareness of assumptions, knowledge and biases that they may be bringing to the research.

Reliable: the capability of a research instrument to consistently produce the same measurements. This can mean calibrating measuring instruments, isolating instruments from external factors that may affect them or devising surveys and questionnaires that can be standardised.

Reliability: the consistency of measurement within research studies that means that results can be reached by other researchers conducting the same experiment under the same conditions to reach the same results.

Research instrument: a means of gathering data from participants. This can be hardware, standardised surveys and questionnaires and researchers who devise and administer interviews or other forms of data collection.

Researcher positionality: the perspectives influenced and formed by the mix of social and political identities taken up by or ascribed to a researcher. Such identities include (but not exclusively) age, class, gender, nationality and sexuality and combine to confer a power-related status on the researcher.

Robust: the ability of a model, test or system to perform effectively when its variables or assumptions are altered or violated.

Secondary data: data collected for a study that is different to the one in which it is currently being used. New questions may be asked of the data in a new study to explore a different research interest.

Social constructionism: an ontology that believes that understanding significance and meaning are created through interactions in the social world. Emphasis is placed on the role of language in constructing what is perceived to be real.

Stakeholder researchers: people or organisations that have an interest in the research, and/or can affect or be affected by its outcomes. They play a role in the research process that can range from sitting on the Advisory Group, through acting as Expert Participants, to helping to ensure that the research is disseminated to appropriate audiences. Their input is valued as having potential to be both supportive and critical.

Suspicious interpretation: the process of exploring data about experience by viewing it through different lenses to seek out what may lie behind the material that is presented.

Theory triangulation: the application of different theories to the interpretation of data that can help to bring different insights and understandings whilst also serving to highlight gaps and contradictions in research conduct and interpretation. It is not necessarily about seeking a convergence of meaning in research.

Transparency: a qualitative research quality criterion that calls for as much as possible to be made available to research audiences. This can include raw data, decisions made in the research process and challenges to its conduct, as well as clear illustrations of how the research was conducted and the findings reached.

Trustworthiness: an evaluation criterion of qualitative research that assesses the transferability, credibility, dependability and confirmability of the research.

Usability: understanding whether research outcomes can be used by a wider audience that may be made up of other researchers, practitioners or others for whom the research outcomes have implications.

Validity: the determination of whether the research truly measures what it claims to measure. Rooted in the positivist approach to research, validity seeks out whether the data gathered, the way in which it has been gathered and the tests and measures applied to it adequately addresses the research question or hypothesis. Internal validity establishes whether the effects identified in research are due to the manipulation of the independent variable. External validity establishes whether the results of the research can be generalised to wider populations or settings.

References

Aron, A., Aron, E. N., Tudor, M., & Nelson, G. (1991). Close relationships as including other in the self. *Journal of Personality and Social Psychology*, *60*(2), 241.

Baiocchi, G. (Ed.). (2003). *Radicals in power: The workers' party and experiments in urban democracy in Brazil*. London: Zed Books.

Bakhtin, M.M. (1981). *The Dialogic Imagination: Four Essays*, Trans. C. Emerson and M. Holquist, ed. M. Holquist. Austin, Texas: University of Texas Press.

Bandura, A. (1997). *Self-efficacy: The exercise of control*. New York: Freeman.

Barkhuus, L., & Polichar, V. E. (2011). Empowerment through seamfulness: Smart phones in everyday life. *Personal and Ubiquitous Computing*, *15*(6), 629–639.

Barnes, D. (1998). Foreword: Looking forward: The concluding remarks at the Castle Conference. *Reconceptualizing Teaching Practice: Self-Study in Teacher Education*, ix–xiv.

Barry, C. A., Britten, N., Barber, N., Bradley, C., & Stevenson, F. (1999). Using reflexivity to optimise teamwork in qualitative research. *Qualitative Health Research, 9*(1), 26–44.

BBC News. (2014). Patient data to be collected from GPs. 6 January, http://www.bbc.co.uk/news/health-25588544.

Berger, R. (2015). Now I see it, now I don't: Researcher's position and reflexivity in qualitative research. *Qualitative Research 15(2):219–234*.

Blass, T. (2004). *The man who shocked the world: The life and legacy of Stanley Milgram* (p. 360). New York: Basic Books.

Bolton, G. (2010). *Reflective practice: Writing and professional development*. Thousand Oaks, CA: Sage Publications.

Bolton, G. (2011). *Write yourself: Creative writing and personal development*. London and Philadelphia: Jessica Kingsley Publishers.

Branney, P. Strickland, C. Darby, F., White, L., & JainS. (2016). Health psychology research using participative mixed qualitative methods and framework analysis: Exploring men's experiences of diagnosis and treatment for prostate cancer. In J. Brooks & N. King (Eds.), *Applied Qualitative Research in Psychology*. London: Palgrave.

Breen, S., McCluskey, A., Meehan, M., O'Donovan, J., & O'Shea, A. (2011). Reflection in practice: The discipline of noticing. In C. Smith (Ed.), *Proceedings of the British society for research into learning mathematics*, Oxford: Oxford University, Vol. 31, November 2011.

Breuer, J. (1955). Fräulein Anna O, Case histories from studies on Hysteria. In Strachey, J. (ed) *The Standard Edition of the Complete Psychological Works of Sigmund Freud, Volume II (1893–1895): Studies on Hysteria* (pp. 19–47), London: The Hogarth Press.

British Psychological Society. (2009). *Code of Ethics and Conduct.* Leicester: British Psychological Society, http://www.bps.org.uk/system/files/documents/code_of_ethics_and_conduct.pdf

British Psychological Society. (2010). *Code of Human Research Ethics.* Leicester: British Psychological Society, http://www.bps.org.uk/sites/default/files/documents/code_of_human_research_ethics.pdf

Brugha, R., & Varvasovszky, Z. (2000). Stakeholder analysis: A review. *Health Policy and Planning, 15*(3), 239–246.

Bruhn, J. (2000). Interdisciplinary research: A philosophy, art form, artefact or antidote?, *Integrative Psychological and Behavioural Science, 35*(1), 58–66.

Bryman, A. (2007). Barriers to integrating quantitative and qualitative research. *Journal of Mixed Methods Research, 1*(1), 8–22.

Burchardt, M. (July 2014). Multiple secularities and cultural memories in Québec. In *XVIII ISA World Congress of Sociology (July 13–19, 2014),* Yokohama, Japan: Isaconf.

Carlson, W., & Wu, J. (2012). The illusion of statistical control: Control variable practice in management research, Organizational Research Methods 15 (3): 413–435.

Carter, D. F., & Hurtado, S. (2007). Bridging key research dilemmas: Quantitative research using a critical eye. *New directions for institutional research, 2007*(133), 25–35.

Caulley, D. N. (2008). Making qualitative research reports less boring: The techniques of writing creative nonfiction. *Qualitative Inquiry.*

Chaudhry, L. N. (1997). Researching 'my people,' researching myself: Fragments of a reflexive tale. *International Journal of Qualitative Studies in Education, 10*(4), 441–453.

Chenail, R. J. (1995). Presenting qualitative data. *The Qualitative Report, 2*(3), 1–8.

Chenail, R. J. (2011). Interviewing the investigator: Strategies for addressing instrumentation and researcher bias concerns in qualitative research. *Qualitative Report, 16*(1), 255–262.

Chevalier-Skolnikoff, S. (1981). The Clever Hans phenomenon, cuing, and ape signing: A Piagetian analysis of methods for instructing animals. *Annals of the New York Academy of Sciences, 364*(1), 60–93.

Clarke, N.J., Caddick, N., & Frost, N.A. (in press). Pluralistic Analysis, in Smith, B.N., & Sparks, A, (eds). The Routledge International Handbook of Qualitative Methods in Sports and Exercise, Routledge.

Coffey, A., & Atkinson, P. (1996). *Making sense of qualitative data: Complementary research strategies.* Thousand Oaks, CA: Sage Publications, Inc.

Colyar, J. (2009). Becoming writing, becoming writers. *Qualitative Inquiry, 15*(2), 421–436.

Cooper, M., & McLeod, J. (2011). Pluralistic Counselling and Psychotherapy, London: Sage Publications.

Cunliffe, A. L., & Karunanayake, G. (2013). Working within hyphen-spaces in ethnographic research implications for research identities and practice. *Organizational Research Methods, 16*(3), 364–392.

Curt, B. C. (1984): *Textuality and tectonics: Troubling social and psychological science*. Buckingham: Open University Press.

David, M., Weiner, G., & Arnot M. (1996). *Feminist approaches to gender equality and schooling in the 1990s*. Paper presented to the AERA Conference, New York.

Davidson, D. (1979). What metaphors mean. In Sheldon Sacks (Ed.), *On Metaphor* (pp. 29–46). Chicago: University of Chicago Press.

Decety, J., & Sommerville, J. A. (2003). Shared representations between self and other: a social cognitive neuroscience view. *Trends in Cognitive Science, 7*(12), 527–533.

Denzin, N. K. & Lincoln, Y. S. (eds.) (1998). *The landscape of qualitative research: Theories and issues*. London: Sage Publications.

Dickson-Swift, V., James, E. L., & Liamputtong, P. (2008). What is sensitive research? In Dickson-Swift, V., James, E.L., & Liamputtong, P. (eds) *Undertaking sensitive research in the health and social sciences: Managing boundaries, emotions and risks* (pp. 1–10), Cambridge University Press.

Dowd, V. (2015). Getting close to my son who died on Air India 182. *BBC News Magazine*, 22 June, http://www.bbc.co.uk/news/magazine-33230091.

DuBois, B. (1983). Passionate scholarship: Notes on values, knowing and method in feminist social sciences. In Gloria Bowles & Renate Duelli Klein (eds.), *Theories of women's studies* (pp. 105–117). London: Routledge and Kegan Paul.

Ellis, C., & Berger, L. (2003). Their story/my story/our story in in Holstein, J. A. & Gubrium, J. F. (eds) *Inside interviewing: New lenses, new concerns* (pp. 467–493), London: Sage Publications.

Finlay, L. (2003). The reflexive journey: Mapping multiple routes. In L. Finlay & B. Gough (eds.), *Reflexivity: A practical guide for researchers in health and social sciences*. Oxford: Blackwell Publishing.

Flax, J. (1990). *Thinking fragments: Psychoanalysis, feminism, and postmodernism in the contemporary West*. Oakland: University of California Press.

Flick, U. (2011). Mixing methods, triangulation and integrated research: Challenges for qualitative research in a world of crisis, In N. Denzin & M. D. Giardina (eds.), *Qualitative inquiry and global crises* (pp. 132–152). Walnut Creek, CA: Left Coast Press Inc.

Frosh, S. (2003). Psychosocial studies and psychology: Is a critical approach emerging? *Human Relations, 56*(12), 1545–1567.

Frost, N. A. (2006). *Taking the other out of mother: The transition to second-time motherhood* (Unpublished thesis). University of London, Birkbeck.

Frost, N. A. (2009). 'Do you know what I mean?': The use of a pluralistic narrative analysis approach in the interpretation of an interview. *Qualitative Research, 9*(1), 9–29.

Frost, N. (ed) (2011). *Qualitative Research Methods in Psychology: Combining Core Approaches,* Open University Press: England and USA.

Frost, N. A., Eatough, V., Shaw, R., Weille, K. L. Tzemou, E., & Baraitser, L. (2012). Pleasure, pain, and procrastination: Reflections on the experience of doing memory-work research. *Qualitative Research in Psychology,* 9(3), 231–248.

Frost, N. A., & Holt, A. (2014). Mother, researcher, feminist, woman: Reflections on 'maternal status' as a researcher identity. *Qualitative Research Journal, 14*(2), 90–102.

Frost, N. A., & Kinmond, K. (2012). Evaluating qualitative research in Sullivan, C., Gibson, S. & Riley, S. (eds) *Doing Your Qualitative Psychology Project,* London: Sage Publications, pp154–172.

Frost, N., & Nolas, S. M. (2013). The contribution of pluralistic qualitative approaches to mixed methods evaluations. *New Directions for Evaluation, 2013*(138), 75–84.

Frost, N., Nolas, S. M., Brooks-Gordon, B., Esin, C., Holt, A., Mehdizadeh, L., & Shinebourne, P. (2010). Pluralism in qualitative research: The impact of different researchers and qualitative approaches on the analysis of qualitative data. *Qualitative Research, 10*(4), 441–460.

Ganga, D., & Scott, S. (May 2006). Cultural 'insiders' and the issue of positionality in qualitative migration research: Moving 'across' and moving 'along' researcher-participant divides. *Forum Qualitative Sozialforschung* [Forum: Qualitative Social Research], 7(3).

Geertz, C. (1975). On the nature of anthropological understanding: Not extraordinary empathy but readily observable symbolic forms enable the anthropologist to grasp the unarticulated concepts that inform the lives and cultures of other peoples. *American Scientist,* 63(1): 47–53.

Gilgun, J. F. (2005). Qualitative research and family psychology. *Journal of Family Psychology, 19*(1), 40.

Gimlin, D., & Throsby, K. (2010). Critiquing thinness and wanting to be thin. In R. Ryan-Flood & R. Gill (eds.), *Secrecy and silence in the research process: Feminist reflections.* New York: Routledge.

Glaser, B. G. (1978). *Theoretical sensitivity: Advances in the methodology of grounded theory* (Vol. 2). Mill Valley, CA: Sociology Press.

Gough, B. (2003). *Reflexivity: A practical guide for researchers in health and social sciences.* Hoboken, NJ: Blackwell Publishing.

Graham, H. (1983). Do her answers fit his questions? Women and the survey method. In E. Gamarnikow, D. Morgan, J. Purvis and D. Taylorson (eds.), *The public and the private* (pp. 132–147). London: Heinemann.

Grbich, C. (2007). *Qualitative data analysis: An introduction.* London: Sage Publications.

Gross, E., & Stone, G. P. (1964). Embarrassment and the analysis of role requirements. *American Journal of Sociology,* 70(1):1–15.

Haahr, A., Norlyk, A., & Hall, E. O. (2013). Ethical challenges embedded in qualitative research interviews with close relatives. *Nursing Ethics,* 0969733013486370.

Haas, P. M. (Ed.). (1992). *Knowledge, power, and international policy coordination.* London: Reaktion Books.

Haraway, D. (1988). Situated knowledges: The science question in feminism and the privilege of partial perspective. *Feminist Studies*, 14(3): 575–599.

Harding, S. (1991). *Strong objectivity and socially situated knowledge.* Cornell University Press.

Harris, L. C., & Ogbonna, E. (2012). Motives for service sabotage: An empirical study of front-line workers. *The Service Industries Journal*, 32(13), 2027–2046.

Haug, F. (1987). *Female sexualization: A collective work of memory* (Trans. Erica Carter). London: Verso.

Hertel, G., Geister, S., & Konradt, U. (2005). Managing virtual teams: A review of current empirical research. *Human Resource Management Review*, 15(1), 69–95.

Hesse-Biber, S. N. (2010). *Mixed methods research: Merging theory with practice.* New York: Guilford Press.

Hesse-Biber, S. (ed.) (2014) *Feminist Research Practice: A Primer*, Sage Publications.

Hesse-Biber, S., Rodriguez, D. & Frost, N.A. (2015). A Qualitatively Driven Approach to Multi Method and Mixed Method Research in Hesse-Biber, S, & Johnson, R.B. (eds) (2015). The Oxford Handbook of Multimethod and Mixed Methods Research Inquiry, Oxford University Press.

Hobson, R. P. (1989). Beyond cognition: A theory of autism. In G. Dawson (Ed.), *Autism: Nature, diagnosis and treatment* (pp. 22–48). New York: Guilford Press.

Hochschild, A. R. (2003). *The managed heart: Commercialization of human feeling.* Oakland: University of California Press.

Hughes, M., McNeish D., Newman T., Roberts H., & Sachdev D. (2000). *What works? Making connections: linking research and practice. A review by Barnardo's Research and Development Team.* Ilford: Barnardo's.

Ito, M., Okabe, D., & Matsuda, M. (2006). *Personal, portable, pedestrian: Mobile phones in Japanese life.* Cambridge: The MIT Press.

James, W. (1913. *Principles of psychology.* New York: Henry Holt.

Janesick, V. J. (2000). The choreography of qualitative research design. *Handbook of Qualitative Research*, 379–399.

Johnson, B., & Macleod Clarke, J. (2003). Collecting sensitive data, the Impact on researchers. *Qualitative Health Research*, 13, 421–434.

Katsiaficas, D., Futch, V. A., Fine, M., & Sirin, S. R. (2011). Everyday hyphens: Exploring youth identities with methodological and analytic pluralism. *Qualitative Research in Psychology*, 8(2), 120–139.

Keenan, R., Horovitz, S., Maki, A., Yamahita, Y., Koizumi, H., & Gore, J. (2002). Simultaneous recording of event-related auditory oddball response using transcranial near infrared optical topography and surface. *EEG Neuroimage, 16*, 587–592.

Kelly, L., Regan, L., & Burton, S. (1992). Defending the indefensible? Quantitative methods and feminist research. In H. Hinds, A. Phoenix, & J. Stacey (eds.), *Working out: New directions in women's studies* (pp. 149–161). Lewes: The Falmer Press.

Kemmis, S., & McTaggart, R. (1988). The action research planner. Victoria, Australia: Deakin University Press.

King, I. (2011). Will Intel finally crack smartphones. *Bloomberg Businessweek June*, 41–42.

King, N., Finlay, L., Ashworth, P., Smith, J. A., Langdridge, D., & Butt, T. (2008). 'Can't really trust that, so what can I trust?': A polyvocal, qualitative analysis of the psychology of mistrust. *Qualitative Research in Psychology*, 5(2), 80–102.

Knapp, S. J., & Van de Creek, L. D. (2006). *Practical ethics for psychologists: A positive approach*. Washington DC: American Psychological Association.

Kuhn, T. S. (1962). *The structure of scientific revolutions*. Chicago, IL: The University of Chicago Press.

LaBoskey, V. K. (2004). The methodology of self-study and its theoretical underpinnings. In *International handbook of self-study of teaching and teacher education practices* (pp. 817–869). The Netherlands: Springer.

Lakoff, G., & Johnson, M. (1980). The metaphorical structure of the human conceptual system. *Cognitive Science*, 4(2), 195–208.

Lavis, V. (2010). Multiple researcher identities: Highlighting tensions and implications for ethical practice in qualitative interviewing. *Qualitative Research in Psychology*, 7(4), 316–331.

Lincoln, Y. S., & Guba, E. G. (1985). Establishing trustworthiness. *Naturalistic Inquiry*, 289, 331.

Lindstrom, M. (2011). You love your iPhone literally. *New York Times*, 1, 21A.

Lings, I., Durden, G., Lee, N., & Cadogan, J. (2010). The role of emotional labour and role stress on burnout and psychological strain in high contact service employees. In *Proceedings of Academy of Marketing Conference 2010*. Coventry University Business School.

Loughran, J., & Northfield, J. (1998). A framework for the development of self-study practice. In Hamilton, M.L. (ed) *Reconceptualizing Teaching Practice: Developing Competence Through Self-Study*, Routledge, pp. 2–18.

Malacrida, C. (2007). Reflexive journaling on emotional research topics: ethical issues for team researchers. *Qualitative Health Research*, 17(10), 1329–1339.

Mark, A., & Snowden, D. (2006). Research Practice or Practicing Research: Innovating Methods in Healthcare. In A. L. Casebeer, A. Harrison & A. Mark (eds.),. Innovations in Health Care: Palgrave Macmillan.

Mason, J. (2002). *Qualitative researching*. Thousand Oaks, CA: Sage.

Mason, J. (2006). Mixing methods in a qualitatively driven way. *Qualitative Research*, 6(1), 9–25.

Mauthner, N. S., & Doucet, A. (2008). 'Knowledge once divided can be hard to put together again' an epistemological critique of collaborative and team-based research practices. *Sociology*, 42(5), 971–985.

Maynard, M. (1994). Methods, practice and epistemology: The debate about feminism and research. In Maynard, M. & Purvis, J. (eds) *Researching women's lives from a feminist perspective*, Taylor & Francis Ltd (p. 26).

McKenna, K. (1991). Subjects of discourse: Learning the language that counts. In Bannerjee, H., Banjeri, E.A. & Himmani, E.B. (eds) *Unsettling relations: The university as a site of feminist struggles* Southend Press, (pp. 109–128).

Meltzoff, A. N., & Brooks, R. (2001). Like me" as a building block for understanding other minds: Bodily acts, attention, and intention. *Intentions and intentionality: Foundations of social cognition*, 171–191.

Merriam, S. B., Johnson-Bailey, J., Lee, M. Y., Kee, Y., Ntseane, G., & Muhamad, M. (2001). Power and positionality: Negotiating insider/outsider status within and across cultures. *International Journal of Lifelong Education*, 20(5), 405–416.

Merton, R. K. (1948). The self-fulfilling prophecy. In Fogarty, Rs (ed) *The Antioch Review*, The Antioch Review Inc, pp. 193–210.

Mies, M. (1983). Towards a methodology for feminist research. In G. Bowles & R. D. Klein (eds.), *Theories of women's studies* (pp. 117–140). London: Routledge and Kegan Paul.

Milgram, S. (1963). Behavioral study of obedience. *Journal of Abnormal and Social Psychology*, 67(4), 371.

Miller, G. (2012). The smartphone psychology manifesto. *Perspectives on Psychological Science*, 7(3), 221–237.

Moore, H.L. (2010). Forms of knowing and un-knowing: secrets about society, sexuality and God in Northern Kenya, in Ryan-Flood, R., & Gill, R. (eds) (2010) *Secrecy and Silence in the Research Process: feminist reflections*, New York, Routledge (pp. 30–41).

Morris, M. E., & Aguilera, A. (2012). Mobile, social, and wearable computing and the evolution of psychological practice. *Professional Psychology: Research and Practice*, 43(6), 622.

Morris, M. E., Kathawala, Q., Leen, T. K., Gorenstein, E. E., Guilak, F., DeLeeuw, W., & Labhard, M. (2010). Mobile therapy: Case study evaluations of a cell phone application for self-awareness. *Journal of Medical Internet Research*, 12(2), e10.

Moss, R. J., Smith, E. B., Anderson, G., Rozenfeld, V,, Evangelista, C., Trahey, C., Venuti, C., & Weiner, E. J. (2014). A survey of key opinion leaders to support curriculum development in advanced medical science liaison training. *Therapeutic Intervention and Regulatory Science*, 49(1): 45–49.

Murphy, M., Dempsey, M., & Halton, C. (2010). Reflective inquiry in social work education. In *Handbook of Reflection and Reflective Inquiry* (pp. 173-188). Springer US.

Neisser, U. (1988). Five kinds of self-knowledge. *Philosophical Psychology*, 1(1), 35–59.

Neisser, U. (1991). Two perceptually given aspects of the self and their development. *Developmental Review*, 11(3), 197–209.

Newman, I., & Benz, C. R. (1998). *Qualitative–quantitative research methodology: Exploring the interactive continuum*. Carbondale: Southern Illinois University Press.

Newcombe, R. (2003). From a client to project stakeholders: A stakeholder mapping approach. *Construction Management and Economics*, 21, 841–848.

Nolas, S. M. (2011). Stories as indicators of practical knowledge: Analysing project workers' talk from a study of participation in a youth inclusion programme. *Journal of Community & Applied Social Psychology*, 21(2), 138–150.

Oakley, A. (1984). *The captured womb: A history of the medical care of pregnant women*. B. Blackwell.

O'Brien, K. (2010). Inside 'doorwork': Gendering the security gaze. In R. Ryan-Flood & R. Gill (eds.), *Secrecy and silence in the research process: Feminist reflections*. New York: Routledge (pp. 117–132).

Ogbonna, E., & Harris, L. C. (2004). Work intensification and emotional labour amongst UK university lecturers: An exploratory study. *Organizational Studies, 25,* 1185–1203.

Onwuegbuzie, A. J. (2003). Effect sizes in qualitative research: A prolegomenon. *Quality and Quantity, 37*(4), 393–409.

Onwuegbuzie, A. J., DaRos, D., & Ryan, J. (1997) The components of statistics anxiety: A phenomenological study. *Focus on Learning Problems in Mathematics, 19*(4), 11–35.

Onwuegbuzie, A. J., & Leech, N. L. (2005). On becoming a pragmatic researcher: The importance of combining quantitative and qualitative research methodologies. *International Journal of Social Research Methodology, 8*(5), 375–387.

Owens, E. (2006). Conversational space and participant shame in interviewing. *Qualitative Inquiry, 12*(6), 1160–1179.

Pajares, F., & Schunk, D. H. (2002). Self and self-belief in psychology and education: A historical perspective. In Aronson, J. (ed) *Improving academic achievement: Impact of psychological factors on education* Academic Press, (pp. 3–21).

Partington, G. (2001). Qualitative research interviews: identifying problems in technique. Issues in Educational Research, 11(2) 32–44.

Partington, D. (2009). *Essential skills for management research*. London: Sage Publications.

Parpart, J. L. (2010). Choosing silence rethinking voice, agency and women's. In R. Ryan-Flood & R. Gill (eds.), *Secrecy and silence in the research process: Feminist reflections*. New York: Routledge (p. 15–29).

Perry, G. (2014). *Behind the shock machine: The untold story of the notorious Milgram psychology experiments*. Scribe Publications, Australia, United Kingdom.

Peshkin, A. (2000). The nature of interpretation in qualitative research. *Educational Researcher, 29*(9), 5–9.

Pezalla, A. E., Pettigrew, J., & Miller-Day, M. (2012). Researching the researcher-as-instrument: An exercise in interviewer self-reflexivity. *Qualitative Research, 12*(2), 165–185.

Phoenix, A. (1991). *Young mothers?* Polity press.

Plato. (2008). *Republic.* New Edition. Oxford: Oxford World's Classics.

Psyography. (2015). Stanley Milgram. http://faculty.frostburg.edu/mbradley/psyography/stanleymilgram.html.

Raver, D. (2015). Stanley Milgram, Psyography:internet source for biographies on psychologists, http://faculty.frostburg.edu/mbradley/psyography/stanleymilgram.html

Reay, D. (2000, February). 'Dim dross': Marginalised women both inside and outside the academy. *Women's Studies International Forum, 23*(1), 13–21.

Reinharz, S. (1983). Experiential analysis: A contribution to feminist research. In Bowles, G. & Klein, R. D (eds)*Theories of Women's Studies*, London: Routledge & Kegan Paul pp 162–191.

Richardson, G. E. (2002). The metatheory of resilience and resiliency. *Journal of Clinical Psychology*, 58(3), 307–321.

Riessman, C. K. (1987). When gender is not enough: Women interviewing women. *Gender & Society*, 1(2), 172–207.

Robins, R. W., Hendin, H. M., & Trzesniewski, K. H. (2001). Measuring global self-esteem: Construct validation of a single-item measure and the Rosenberg Self-Esteem Scale. *Personality and Social Psychology Bulletin*, 27(2), 151–161.

Ricoeur, P. (1996). Figuring the sacred. *Theological Studies*, 57, 545–546.

Riessman, C. K. (19987. When gender is not enough: women interviewing women, *Gender & Society*, 9(2):172–207.

Rogers, Y., Scaife, M., & Rizzo, A. (2005). Interdisciplinarity: An emergent or engineered process. In Derry, S.J., Schon, C.D. & Gernsbacher, M.A (eds) *Interdisciplinary collaboration: An emerging cognitive science* Laurence Erlbaum Associates, Inc (pp. 265–283).

Rosenthal, M. L. (1967). *The new poets: American and British poetry since World War II* (Vol. 188). New York: Oxford University Press.

Rosenthal, S. H. (1964). Persistent hallucinosis following repeated administration of hallucinogenic drugs. *American Journal of Psychiatry*, 121(3), 238–244.

Rosenthal, R. (1963). On the social psychology of the psychological experiment: 1, 2 the experimenter's hypothesis as unintended determinant of experimental results. *American Scientist*, 268–283 Vol. 51 (2).

Rosenthal, R. (1966). Experimenter effects in behavioral research. East Norwalk, CT, US: Appleton-Century-Crofts.

Rosenthal, R., & Jacobson, L. (1968). *Pygmalion in the classroom: Teacher expectation and pupils' intellectual development*. New York: Holt, Rinehart and Winston.

Ross, J. (2009). *Was that infinity or affinity? Qualitative research transcription as translation*. Draft, 4, 1–14. Retrieved September 12, 2011, from http://jenrossity.net/blog/wpcontent/uploads/2009/03/ross2009_affinityinfinity_v4.pdf

Roth, W. M. (March 2006). Collective responsibility and solidarity: Toward a body-centered ethics. *Forum Qualitative Sozialforschung* [Forum: Qualitative Social Research], 7(2).

Rothman, S., Lipset, S. M., & Nevitte, N. (2003). Rothman, S., Lipset, S. M., & Nevitte, N. (2003). Does enrollment diversity improve university education?. *International Journal of Public Opinion Research*, 15(1), 8–26.

Runyan, J. D., Steenbergh, T. A., Bainbridge, C., Daugherty, D. A., Oke, L., & Fry, B. N. (2013). A smartphone ecological momentary assessment/intervention 'app' for collecting real-time data and promoting self-awareness. *PloS one*, 8(8), e71325.

Russell, G. M., & Kelly, N. H. (2002). Research as interacting dialogic processes: Implications for reflexivity. *Forum: Qualitative Social Research*, 3(3) Art 18.

Ryan, L., & Golden, A. (2006). 'Tick the box please': A reflexive approach to doing quantitative social research. *Sociology*, 40(6), 1191–1200.

Ryan, L., Leavey, G., Golden, A., Blizard, R., & King, M. (2006). Depression in Irish migrants living in London: case–control study. *The British Journal of Psychiatry*, 188(6), 560–566.

Ryan-Flood, R., & Gill, R. (eds.). (2010). *Secrecy and silence in the research process: feminist reflections*. New York: Routledge.

Samaras, A. P. (2011). *Self-study teacher research: Improving your practice through collaborative inquiry*. Thousand Oaks, CA: Sage Publications.

Samaras, A. P., & Freese, A. R. (2006). *Self-study of teaching practices primer*. New York: Peter Lang.

Sampson, H., Bloor, M., & Fincham, B. (2008). A price worth paying? Considering the 'cost' of reflexive research methods and the influence of feminist ways of doing'. *Sociology, 42*(5), 919–933.

Scott, S., Hinton-Smith, T., Härmä, V., & Broome, K. (2012). The reluctant researcher: Shyness in the field. *Qualitative Research*, 1468794112439015.

Schunk, S., & Russell, T. (2005). Self-study, critical friendship and the complexities of teacher education. *Studying Teacher Education, 1*(2), 107–121.

Scottish Development Centre for Mental Health and the Research Unit in Health, Behaviour and Change. (2005). Written on the body: A review of literature on self-cutting prepared for the National Inquiry into Self Harm among Young People: executive summary.

Sebeok, T. A., & Rosenthal, R. E. (1981). The Clever Hans phenomenon: Communication with horses, whales, apes, and people. *Annals of the New York Academy of Sciences, Vol 364 pp309*.

Shinebourne, P. (2011). Interpretative phenomenological analysis. In N. A. Frost (Ed.), *Qualitative research in psychology: Combining core approaches*. Open University Press: England, New York.

Slatin, C., Galizzi, M., Devereaux Melillo, K., & Mawn, B. (2004). Conducting interdisciplinary research to promote healthy and safe employment in health care: Promises and pitfalls. *Public Health Reports, 119*, 60–72.

Smith, J. A., Flowers, P., & Larkin, M. (2009). *Interpretative phenomenological analysis: Theory, method and research*. Thousand Oaks, CA: Sage.

Spandler, H. (1996). *Who's hurting who?: Young people, self-harm and suicide*, 42nd Street Steffen, E., & Coyle, A. (2010). Can 'sense of presence' experiences in bereavement be conceptualised as spiritual phenomena? *Mental Health, Religion & Culture, 13*(3), 273–291.

Steffen, E., & Coyle, A. (in press 2015). 'I thought they should know … that daddy is not completely gone': A case study of sense-of-presence experiences in bereavement and family meaning-making. *Omega: Journal of Death and Dying*.

Sullivan, G. (2012). *Qualitative Data Analysis: Using a Dialogical Approach*, London: Sage Publications.

Tarpey, M. (2011). Public involvement in research applications to the National Research Ethics Service. *INVOLVE, Eastleigh*.Taylor, R. S. (1962). The process of asking questions. *American Documentation, 13*(4), 391–396.

Taylor, R. S. (1986). *Value added processes in information systems*. Norwood, NJ: Ablex Publishing Corporation.

Trevarthen, C. (1979). Communication and cooperation in early infancy: A description of primary intersubjectivity. In Bullowa, M. (ed) *Before speech: The beginning of interpersonal communication* Cambridge: Cambridge University Press, pp. 321–347.

Turato, E. R. (2005). Métodos qualitativos e quantitativos na área da saúde: definições, diferenças e seus objetos de pesquisa Qualitative and quantitative methods in health: definitions, differences and research subjects. *Rev Saúde Pública*, *39*(3), 507–514.

Van Manen, M. (1990). *Researching lived experience: Human science for an action sensitive pedagogy*. State University of New York Press, USA.

Varvasovszky, Z., & Mckee, M. (1998). An analysis of alcohol policy in Hungary. Who is in charge?. *Addiction*, *93*(12), 1815–1827.

Walt, G., Shiffman, J., Schneider, H., Murray, S. F., Brugha, R., & Gilson, L. (2008). 'Doing' health policy analysis: methodological and conceptual reflections and challenges. *Health Policy and Planning*, *23*(5), 308–317.

Warner, S., & Spandler, H. (2012). New strategies for research in clinical practice: A focus on self-harm. *Qualitative Research in Psychology*, *9*, 13–26.

Weinstock, D., & Kahane, D. (2010). Introduction. In D. Weinstock, D. Kahane, D. Leydet, & M. Williams (eds.), *Deliberative democracy in practice* (pp. 1–18). Vancouver: University of British Columbia Press.

Westmarland, N. (February 2001). The quantitative/qualitative debate and feminist research: A subjective view of objectivity. *Forum Qualitative Sozialforschung* [Forum: Qualitative Social Research], *2*(1).

Westmarland, N., & Anderson, J. (2001). Safe at the wheel? Security issues for female taxi drivers: Visions of a feminine future. *The Security Journal*, *14*(2), 29–40.

Whitehead, J., & McNiff, J. (2006). *Action research: Living theory*. Thousand Oaks, CA: Sage Publications.

Wilkinson, S. (1988, December). The role of reflexivity in feminist psychology. *Women's Studies International Forum*, *11*(5), 493–502.

Willig, C. (2012). *Qualitative interpretation and analysis in psychology*. Buckingham: Open University Press.

Zinn, J. O. (2006). Recent developments in sociology of risk and uncertainty. Zinn, J. O. (2006, January). Recent Developments in Sociology of Risk and Uncertainty. In *Forum: Qualitative Social Research* (Vol. 7, No. 1).

Index